CLOSED CURTAIN

Lives of de Wallen

WRITTEN BY BRUCE HARRIS

ILLUSTRATED BY MICHELLE BIRD

WHITE
BOUCKE
PUBLISHING
LAFAYETTE, COLORADO

Cover illustration by Michelle Bird

First published October 2001

ISBN 1-888580-16-X

Printed in the United States of America

Library of Congress Cataloging-in-Publication Data

Harris, Bruce, 1946-
    Closed curtain : lives of de wallen / written by Bruce Harris ; illustrated by Michelle
Bird.
       p. cm.
    ISBN 1-88858016-X
    1. Prostitution--Netherlands--Amsterdam. 2. Sex-oriented businesses--Netherlands-
       Amsterdam. I. Bird, Michelle. II. Title.

HQ213.A4 H37 2001
306.74'09492'352--dc21   2001045512

WHITE
BOUCKE
PUBLISHING
PO BOX 400, LAFAYETTE, CO 80026, USA

www.white-boucke.com

Dedications & Appreciations

Many Dutch citizens and members of Amsterdam's international community were of great help in the development and evolution of *Closed Curtain*. When the prototype version was put together, I was living in a hostel, then a waterfront canal barge, without computer or work space, so a lot of the work was done in pubs, coffeeshops, and Internet cafes. This often led to acquaintanceships which gave me added insight on, or amusing anecdotes about, our subject matter. Add the folks who were kind enough to examine the work in progress and lend helpful criticism, and it is understandable if we've accidentally omitted someone who should be listed below.

All the staff and regulars at the *Jolly Joker* coffeeshop, where it all began, and from whom we received ongoing encouragement over weary months. Also, all the folks at the *Juicebar Coffeeshop Betty Boop*, who were equally helpful.

Ivan Ramphal, owner of *Ivan's Ship Shop*, on whose ship *Closed Curtain* was mostly written, and who was our first distributor, and the staff of the *Café Pollux* for encouragement and too much *jenever* gin.

Suzanne Blanchard, for reading, insight, and a fine photographic eye.

Lizzie McDowell-Forsyth, the munchkin queen of Amsterdam's street musicians, who declared us "brilliant" before we were.

Owen Liebreich, old "Stones 'n' Bones," for encouragement and prayer.

Ken and Janet Ricci of the *American Music Project* in New York, Paula Helene of Point Richmond, California, and June Field of *Poker Digest* magazine in Las Vegas, all of whom somehow worked together to get me the small pay checks which enabled me to complete the writing.

Steve Egan, an American jock in Amsterdam, for logistical support, and Eric Vallaster for helping us keep our project before the public. He made me a pallet on his floor and the promise of an eternal ass-kicking if I gave up. Baldwin van de Helm, Michelle's life partner, who tolerated the disruption in his life caused by our collaboration, and for our maps.

Michelle herself, for wielding a mean whip.

And to my father, Dr. Paul Harris, who would have loved *de Wallen*.

Photo Credits

"Amsterdam, by its tolerance for unconventional behavior, attracts crazy people. Holland is a conventional country; crazy people have to go somewhere. They go to the capital, where the lovely canals, thousands of gable houses, hundreds of bridges of every shape and form, lines of old trees, clusters of offbeat bars and cafes, dozens of cinemas and theaters, encourage and protect the odd. Crazy people are special people. They carry the country's genius, its urge to create, to find new ways. The State smiles and is proud of its crazy people. But the State does not approve of anarchism. It limits the odd."

Janwillem van de Wetering
Death of a Hawker
(W&L Books, Amsterdam)

CONTENTS

INTRODUCTION

Amsterdam is the only European travel destination in which the Red-Light District is as popular a tourist attraction as shopping areas, museums, churches, and palaces. Yet, until now, there has been no guide in English to help visitors fully enjoy the wonders of this unique and historic section of one of the continent's most beautiful cities. The book you are holding is the first to give English speakers the essential background to enhance the experience of a stroll through Amsterdam's most exciting neighborhood.

Closed Curtain was born in the Red Light. The artist and photographer, Michelle Bird, was working a day job at the Jolly Joker coffeeshop, on Nieuwmarkt square, just a half-block from the first window brothels of *de Wallen*. This is the Dutch name for the Red-Light District, referring to the medieval walls, or more properly ramparts which, as we'll see in the next chapter, were cities' defenses in centuries past, when *de Wallen* was Amsterdam. Another name for the Red-Light District is *de Rosse Buurt*, which translates as "the pink (or rose) neighborhood."

During slow periods, Michelle had produced a series of pen-and-ink drawings of the ebb and flow of pathos and comedy passing by the coffeeshop day by day. When she showed them to me, I was struck by the way she'd captured the nonchalant prurience of *de Wallen* and depicted many of its characters as reflecting a sad humanity, warped by excess. At times, she shows us implied depravity in a manner which does not shock or disgust, but rather arouses a disapproving compassion in the viewer. We decided to add text and photos to her drawings and share our observations of this outrageous and charming neighborhood.

Our first task was to find out what else was available in the bookstores and souvenir shops. We were surprised to find that there was apparently no other book in print in English which gave more than a cursory view of the more obvious attractions of the *Rosse Buurt*.

At first glance, it may seem odd for two Americans to produce a book on a unique Amsterdam phenomenon, and we were ourselves surprised when none of the locals we spoke to questioned our credentials or, later, had anything but compliments for the thirty-two-page portfolio we self-published in late 2000.

We each bring an informed perspective to our subject. Michelle has lived and worked in the Netherlands for over ten years, three of them as a salesperson in red-light cannabis coffeeshops. I first visited Amsterdam in 1966, for a four-month stay, and have been spending progressively longer periods here over the past four years, easing into full-time residence. In addition, we share a common background in having lived many years in the San Francisco Bay Area of California. San Francisco is, in many ways, America's Amsterdam: sexually and politically liberal, the gay capital of the country, and home to North Beach—as close to *de Wallen* as you'll find in the States (with "massage parlors" instead of window brothels). I also had the youthful experience of working two years in a prostitution hotel in what was then New York's red-light district. As a journalist, I've visited Hamburg's St. Pauli district, Europe's other famous ancient center for open prostitution and other libertine activities.

The prototype *Closed Curtain* was well-received in our test markets; the next step was to find a publisher for a formal, expanded edition. We had read and enjoyed *The UnDutchables,* an essential and hilarious guide for foreigners learning to live among the Dutch, by Colin White and Laurie Boucke, so their publishing house seemed a natural for our first query (these two longtime residents of the Netherlands now publish a line of other works). We were delighted that they were interested in working with *Closed Curtain* (coincidentally, a project they had also long wished to realize), which we hope you also enjoy and which—unlike so many lewd or tacky keepsakes from a tour of *de Wallen*—you can take home and show to your maiden Aunt Tillie without fear of her inducing cardiac arrest.

De Wallen is an area of just twenty-some blocks radiating from the brick colossus of the Oude Kerk (Old Church), the oldest monument in Amsterdam, a ten-minute walk from the central railway station. For over three hundred years, this has been the center for Amsterdam's lively, open sex trade. First-time visitors strolling through the district's streets and alleyways are usually taken aback, no matter how well prepared, at first sight of the endless array of scantily clad "ladies in the windows," the sex boutiques, live shows, erotic cinemas, and porno shops. Add the casinos, crowded pubs, cafes, and marijuana-selling coffeeshops, and it all seems a Disneyland of vice, down to the street-corner drug dealers hawking their wares and the kneeling Three-Card Monte dealers (*balletje-balletje*: same game, using a hidden ball instead of playing cards) in the alleys.

But the citizens and denizens of the Red Light are real people living in a bizarre environment where normal families rear their young in flats above *raambordelen* (window brothels), congregate in traditional Dutch "brown bars" (pubs with brown paneling and generations of nicotine stains on the walls), and walk to Sunday services at the Oude Kerk, past people smoking hashish on the *terras* (sidewalk cafe) of the nearby Old Church Coffeeshop and the working girls in the windows for whom it is, after all, just another shift. In these pages, you'll meet the people who live, work, and "shop" in *de Wallen*, some "in the life" (of prostitution) or on its fringes, some not, and learn something of the history and evolution of Amsterdam's first *buurt* (neighborhood).

We'll also explore some unusual aspects (for foreigners) of Dutch and, more specifically, Amsterdam culture and traditions which make the Red-Light District so sensational to visitors from around the world, but which just define another one of the city's patchwork of distinctive neighborhoods to those who live here.

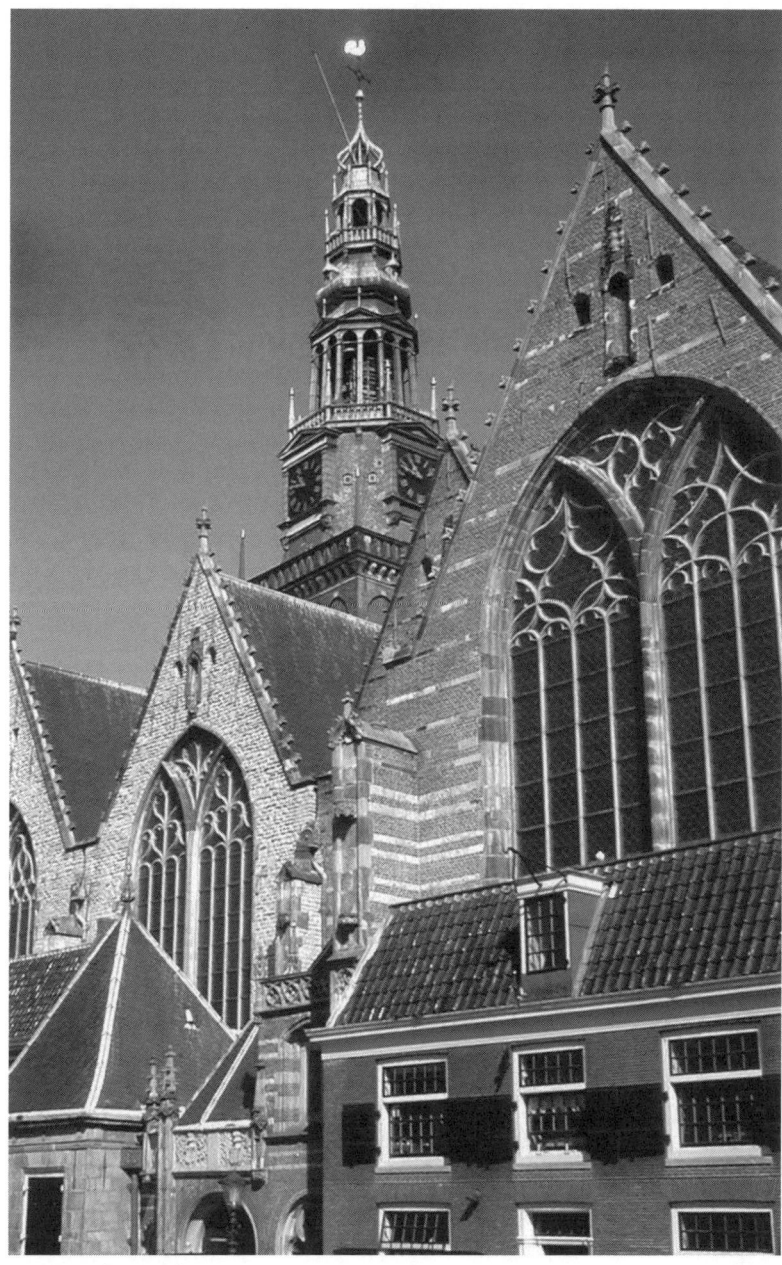

De Oude Kerk

Whether you read this book before or after an excursion to the Red Light, in the comfort of your hotel room or in the departure lounge at Schiphol Airport, we hope you enjoy our take on lives of *de Wallen* and come back for another taste of the glories of Amsterdam.

THE LAY OF DE WALLEN

Before we get into what goes on in *de Wallen*, let's take a brief look at the geography of the area. The Red Light is traversed north-south by two lovely canals, bisecting two parallel streets, Oudezijds Voorburgwal and Oudezijds Achterburgwal, which served this original old city of Amsterdam. The canals are crossed by a series of classic wrought-iron bridges. Walking around the Old City, you'll rarely see a vehicle bigger than a small delivery truck. Even the fire department has scaled-down hook-and-ladder trucks to operate on the ancient narrow streets and alleyways.

If you're lucky, you'll see a not unusual spectacle occurring when large commercial vehicles, or even tour buses, blunder from the wider streets outside the district, then flounder about trying to figure out how to turn around. I once saw a lost cement mixer make twenty attempts to make a U-turn over the narrow Oudekennisbrug (Old Acquaintance Bridge), the driver and assistant working frantically to get out of the neighborhood before the *politie* (police) showed up, accompanied by a chorus of laughing spectators. They finally made it without damaging the metalwork of the bridge railings, but crushed several bicycles which were chained to them, a fact they did not point out to the cops who finally stopped them a block away. Crushed bicycles are a common sight and, since thousands of bikes are stolen in the city every week, and a couple hundred more fished out of the canals, you'll notice that almost no one in Amsterdam rides one of any value.

From the canals, the Red Light stretches one block to the east, bordering on Nieuwmarkt square and the meandering Zeedijk, the official oldest street in Amsterdam. Walk west, and you'll come to Warmoesstraat, which many neighborhood residents insist is really the oldest street in the city. Centuries ago, the street was the home of the vegetable market (*warmoes* meant "vegetables" in medieval Dutch). Today, it is the location of most of the gay clubs in *de Wallen*. You'll find window brothels scattered all over the neighborhood, with possibly the greatest concentration in the streets and alleys around the Oude Kerk.

But, if you can lift your eyes from the ground-floor panoply of sex shops, strip clubs, live shows, and scantily clad lasses, you'll see classic

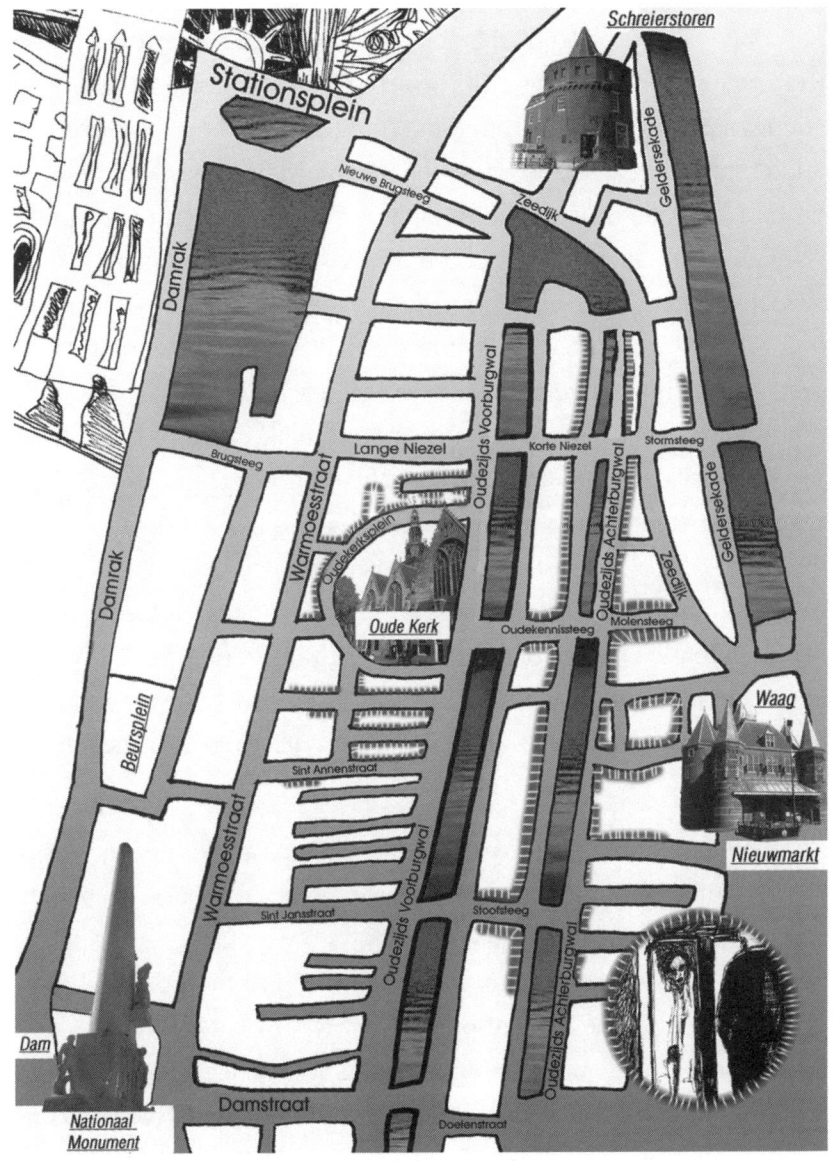

De Wallen

Dutch seventeenth- and eighteenth-century architecture, houses erected when *de Wallen* was the heart of Amsterdam and the wealthy part of town, protected by the ancient city walls. Several towers from the original fortifications still form borders of the Red Light. The Nieuwmarkt is centered around de Waag, built in 1488 as a city gate and customs house in the days when Amsterdam was a key member of the Hanseatic League, the medieval trade confederation of northern European cities which led the transition of the continent from a feudal agricultural economy to early mercantile capitalism. It is now a comfortable restaurant, with Internet access and a reading table stocked with major international publications. But de Waag has served many functions over the centuries: guild hall; place of execution; medical facility (Rembrandt painted *The Anatomy Lesson* there); and center of a holding area for Jews being shipped to their deaths during the Nazi occupation. Just down Geldersekade, across from the current waterfront of the river IJ, is the Schreierstoren (crier's tower), where Henrik (Henry) Hudson departed on his voyage to discover New York and claim it for the Dutch Republic, and from which the tearful families of overdue mariners would gather for a glimpse of homecoming sails.

When the sun hits the narrow, tile rooftops and distinct gables of the canal houses, and reflects off the painted brick facades, it's easy to imagine the waterways of *de Wallen* clogged with barges bringing the riches of empire to the city's warehouses and to the powerful merchants who built the elegant homes which now cater to what some would call a baser obsession than gold. It was only in the late seventeenth century that the wealthy *burgers* of the city, becoming ever richer, built the newer, finer houses on the outer canals and abandoned *de Wallen* to working-class residents and purveyors of vice.

De Waag

De Schreierstoren

Other attractions of the neighborhood include the stately campus of the University of Amsterdam, which anchors the southern end of the Red Light, the old *beurs* (stock exchange) west of Warmoesstraat, the sidewalk cafes and flower carts of the Nieuwmarkt, and the shops and restaurants of Amsterdam's small Chinatown. If you walk down Geldersekade from de Waag to the Schreierstoren, look to your left, and you'll see a small stretch of perhaps eight staffed windows separated from the rest of the Red Light by the Zeedijk, a remnant of the days before that ancient street was "gentrified," cutting the ladies off from their colleagues in *de Wallen* proper.

Although the Zeedijk was once the haunt of dealers, *junks* (junkies), and *tippelaars* (streetwalkers), efforts to force these undesirables into less trafficked areas and restore the Zeedijk to its former glory have been largely successful. Today, although the window brothels start a few meters west of the narrow, meandering street, the Zeedijk itself is lined with a tempting array of restaurants offering Chinese, Thai, Surinamese, and European cuisines, as well as brown bars, stores selling Asian and African arts and crafts, oriental food marts, and other specialty shops. One relatively new landmark of the Zeedijk is the lovely Fo Kuang Shan Buddhist temple just a hundred meters down from the Nieuwmarkt. Opened with great pomp and ceremony in July 2000, with Queen Beatrix and Prince Claus in attendance, the temple is an excellent place to take a few minutes to meditate before plunging back out into the Red Light. Further down the street, you'll see the Nachtbar San Francisco, which opens each night at midnight and is a good place to see neighborhood folks—"straight" and otherwise—relaxing at the close of a long Red-Light day.

Zeedijk Shadows

WHY IS AMSTERDAM
DIFFERENT?

The world is full of red-light districts. Whether prostitution is really the oldest profession is open to debate, much like the chicken and the egg riddle. The first client, after all, had to first earn whatever he paid for his pleasure. Today, whether legal or not, the venerable venereal trade, and its contingent vices, continue to thrive in all great cities, with a few exceptions (Salt Lake City and the Vatican come to mind). Why, then, is Amsterdam's the only city center of vice which draws hordes of visitors who come, not to sample the wares of *de Wallen*, but just to gawk at the ladies in the windows (*raamvrouwen* in Dutch)? They leave plenty of money in *de buurt* (the neighborhood) through purchases of souvenirs, the odd "novelty," pornography they can't get at home, or by taking one of the Red-Light tours offered by several operators. But I doubt that many of the tourists who have the Red-Light District high on their Amsterdam "must see" lists would be caught dead taking a leisurely stroll through their own cities' sex entertainment neighborhoods.

Of course, the fact that prostitution is legal here has something to do with the nature of *de Wallen*. In other countries, where the trade is criminal, the nitty-gritty street variety is usually concentrated, by police tactics, to marginal areas where it won't spill over into respectable residential neighborhoods. In such cases, sex workers and their satellite cohorts, the pimps, porn peddlers, muggers, and other hangers-on, are segregated from the general population. Prostitutes (*prostituees* in Dutch) and others are subject to random arrest to keep them in line and under control and are vulnerable to being forced to relocate at the whim of any politician vowing to "clean up the city."

I worked my way through college as a night clerk in a seedy welfare hotel cum whorehouse in the heart of the Tenderloin, then Manhattan's red-light district. Prostitution is strictly illegal in New York, and the campaigns of Mayor Rudy Guilliani in the 1990s have all but eliminated the raunchier sex businesses from Midtown. In the sixties, the girls worked the streets from Broadway to the Hudson River, from

Painted Door in de Wallen

Red-Light Souvenirs

Times Square to the Theater District, and, although there were a few who had been around for many years, turnover was generally high. Unlike *de Wallen*, which is full of families and old folk, the Tenderloin had little conventional housing, and what there was belonged to the pimps and their stables, or overflowed with multigenerational welfare families. Otherwise, it was mostly rundown hotels, bars, topless joints, and peep shows. Life for the hookers, pimps, junkies, and even less savory residents of the neighborhood was brutish, tawdry, and often violently cut short.

Where criminal sanctions are enforced, there is little protection available from the guardians of law and order, for either the sellers or the buyers. I once had to translate for two Midtown NYPD beat cops trying to get a statement from a Chilean seaman who had taken two girls to one of our deluxe $8 Tenderloin love nests. Not only had he received no services, but he had also been stung for his cash, passport, and savings book. When the officers tired of trying to explain the procedure for filing a complaint to the bellicose, drunken mariner, the sergeant closed his report book, and they both turned to go. "Look kid," one said, "tell him he came to get laid and got f—ked instead."

So, the legality of sex for sale in Amsterdam certainly creates a more open and secure environment for all. It also fosters a more positive relationship with the police, who ensure that providers of services and merchants obey *de regels* ("the rules," which, as we'll see, are central to every aspect of Dutch life), so that clients and tourists alike can enjoy high spirits and low behavior in safety.

It is more than just the illicit pleasures available on all sides that distinguishes *de Wallen*. Hamburg's St. Pauli district, surrounding the infamous Reeperbahn, is also a centuries-old legal red-light district, about the size of *de Wallen*. But St. Pauli is almost totally devoted to sex and other entertainment businesses. There, dozens of half-naked streetwalkers crowd the sidewalk just across the street from the forbidding Reeperbahn *Polizei* headquarters, and window brothels are everywhere. There are also, to be sure, restaurants, music clubs, and other legitimate attractions in St. Pauli; *Cats* has been playing there for years. But you won't see, as you do in Amsterdam, women with shopping bags, kids in tow, chatting on the street around the corner from rows of windows showcasing ladies for rent. As opposed to the violent criminality of the Tenderloin or the unrelieved licentiousness of St. Pauli, the ambiance of *de Wallen* forms an integral part of the overall character of Amsterdam rather than serving as a segregated "combat zone" for practitioners of depravity. Those visiting for the first time in the daylight hours are often surprised by the bustle of ordinary citizens, families, working men, and business types going about their normal affairs. One friend, visiting from the States, expressed surprise at "how tame it is." On foot and bicycle, dancing Amsterdam's intricate mix of street ballet and bullfighting moves, the locals ignore the throngs of gaping tourists and pay no mind to the exotic treats on all sides, which are, after all, only one feature of the neighborhood.

I think it is this coexistence of a "normal" community with the sex businesses, bars, coffeeshops, and gambling houses which lends the neighborhood a unique piquant charm, a more appealing glow than I've seen in other red-light districts. One illustration of this dichotomy can be found right in the middle of it all, at the Oude Kerk. This massive citadel to God has been a center of Amsterdam's spiritual life, first Catholic, then Dutch Reformed, since 1304. In addition to being open to visitors for tours and concerts, it still offers, as I've mentioned, Sunday afternoon worship services. The three-quarter circle of the cobble-stoned Oudekerksplein (the street surrounding the church) is lined on the side opposite with almost nonstop window brothels, coffeeshops, bars, two sex cinemas, a "window" rental agency, and the Prostitution Information Center (Prostitutie Informatie Centrum). Tucked in the middle of all this sin, you'll find the Princess Juliana Child Care Center.

A few blocks north of the Oude Kerk, at Oudezijds Voorburgwal 14, Amsterdam's oldest brick building is also the Red-Light headquarters of the Salvation Army (Leger des Heils), the busiest of the soul-saving groups working the neighborhood. In addition to providing postal addresses for street people and intake to social services, the Sally operates an 80-bed hostel for the homeless and a housing complex for pensioners. The Army chapel, one of several outreach missions offering religious services and Bible study in *de Wallen*, is at Oudezijds Achterburgwal 45 where, in true Red-Light style, it is located between the Royal Taste Hotel Bar and a row of very popular windows.

Another of my favorite Red-Light Kodak moments took place at the Nieuwmarkt end of Monnikenstraat (Monk's Street). The first half of this narrow block-long passageway is home to small neighborhood businesses—a laundromat, a Middle Eastern restaurant, a tobacconist. It was a lovely spring day, and three precious little girls, perhaps ten years old, were playing a game similar to hopscotch in front of the mom-and-pop corner delicatessen. They were in a circle in the mouth of the lane, laughing and skipping like an Amsterdam incarnation of a Norman Rockwell scene, innocence personified. Over their heads, I could see the steady beacons of the fluorescents over the windows of what I call the "Alley of the Blondes," the second half of Monnikenstraat, eastern border of the Red Light.

Window Dressing

The Pinockio "Woody" Club

The Oude Kerk also mounts regular art and photography exhibits and can be rented for special events. An acquaintance of mine was working for the church a few years back when a giant American entertainment company with a decidedly "family values" image rented it for a celebration of the opening of a new film. Their advance men were shocked to discover that their guests, in walking from the canal boats delivering them to the church, would have to pass almost a dozen half-naked prostitutes working in the windows. Fortunately, the girls were willing to close their curtains during the crucial time period—for three times the going rate! I'm sure most party guests, certainly the Europeans, knew what was up, but I can imagine Aunt Tillie reporting to her bridge club back home, "And, my dears, the Dutch are so quaint. There was a whole row of glass-front doors, and all the curtain designs were coordinated."

We'll be delving into many aspects of prostitution, drug policies, other sex businesses, and gambling in our exploration of *de Wallen*, as well as the history and classic building stock, which add yet another dimension to the neighborhood. As you make your way through the area, keep your eyes open for signs of the thriving community of working-class families, students, and professionals—all just plain folks who add to the charm and laid-back ambience which distinguishes Amsterdam's Red-Light District from any other.

GEDOGEN:
REGULATED TOLERANCE

How can all this be legal? We hear many visitors exclaim this as they gape at *de Wallen's* cornucopia of taboo delights. The answer is that it is and it isn't. Dutch law contains a unique doctrine called *gedogen,* or "regulated tolerance." This unusual way of applying the law would probably not work in any other country. Many foreigners think that, because gambling, prostitution, pornography, and soft drug use are openly tolerated, the Dutch, and particularly Amsterdammers, are a race of sex-obsessed dope fiends. This view of Amsterdammers is, ironically, shared by most of the rest of Holland. But the Netherlands is in many ways one of the most conservative and regulated cultures in Europe, as well as the one which most values individual freedom, within accepted limits.

The Dutch take great pride in having a government based on consensus. A culture which survived and evolved in an inhospitable climate, claiming its living space from the sea, and built a global empire while fighting off outside enemies, had to produce individuals who could rely on their fellow citizens to respect their personal "space," but who would also pitch in as a team when the group was threatened. This "polder mentality," so called for the muddy moors upon which much of the nation is built, would seem to be one reason *gedogen* works. Some also suggest that the national feeling that "the only thing we don't tolerate is intolerance" is a residue of guilt stemming from the Calvinism of the established Dutch Reformed Church.

Regardless of its source, *gedogen* can only work in a culture with a highly developed understanding of the social contract between a state and the people it governs, one which is respected by both government officials and ordinary citizens. Businesses may be *gedoogd* (tolerated) if, in the judgment of the public prosecutor's office and the police (both often using studies and recommendations produced by foundations formed to advise them), the social and/or economic costs of strictly enforcing laws against their operation would be greater than the alternative of tolerating them under strict regulation. This permits the authorities to impose informal laws and regulations under which certain otherwise-illegal activities will be tolerated, and to change "the rules" to respond to problems without resorting to ponderous legislative procedure.

The issue of prostitution is more complex than some other tolerated behaviors. No one can deny that the flesh trade produces its victims. The globalization of the traffic in women coerced into "the life" is an appalling reality which has extended its tentacles to the Netherlands (the Foundation Against the Trade in Women, or Stichting Tegen Vrouwenhandel, in Utrecht is devoted to the plight of these unfortunate women), although perhaps to a lesser degree than in countries where prostitution is illegal. Prostitutes here have organizations and foundations (*stichtingen*), such as Stichting de Rode Draad (Red Thread Foundation), the so-called prostitutes' union, to help them understand and secure their rights. The Dutch have always recognized that it is impractical to take a strict prohibitionist attitude towards a profession it is impossible to eliminate. Working girls have been tolerated in Amsterdam since the fifteenth century and concentrated in *de Wallen* since the seventeenth. Degrees of tolerance and regulations have varied. Local lore has it that the origin of the Red Light was an ancient requirement that streetwalkers carry red candles to advertise their availability. In the nineteenth century, prostitutes were required to carry licenses as *publieke vrouwen* (public women).

In 1911, the practice of prostitution was made legal, after centuries of *gedogen*. Trading in women, however, as a pimp or brothel-keeper, remained illegal, with stiff penalties. But such "managers" perform essential jobs in the business, providing prostitutes places to work, steering clients to them, and providing protection from unruly or dissatisfied customers. They were tolerated so long as they obeyed the rules.

In addition to the Red Thread and the Prostitution Information Center, the Dutch government funds the Mr A. de Graaf Foundation to study and make recommendations on issues of prostitution. The foundation provides assistance to a number of other organizations, such as halfway houses for women who want to get out of the business, and publishes periodicals and books for the public and professionals. If you want an excellent overview of the history of prostitution in Amsterdam, de Graaf staffers Marieke van Doorninck and Margol Jongedijk have written an excellent book, *In Het Leven* (*In the Life*), available at the Prostitution Information Center. Although the book is in Dutch, it is profusely illustrated with period prints giving a visual presentation of four centuries of prostitution in the city.

The foundation was also instrumental in the last major change in prostitution law in the Netherlands. On October 1, 2000, after decades *gedoogd*, brothels and sex clubs became fully legal. At the same time, criminal penalties for coercing women into the business, or otherwise trading in flesh except as a legal employer, were increased dramatically. The intent of the new law was to impose standard working conditions for employees of sex businesses, such as adequate security, reasonable hours and pay, washable walls in brothel rooms, and full coverage by the social welfare system, as well as to make it more difficult for "white slavers" to place their merchandise. One impetus for the change was the report of a parliamentary committee in the 1990s which identified approximately sixteen gangs controlling the economy of "tolerated" legal and illegal businesses through intimidation and violence. According to Chrisje Brants of the University of Utrecht Faculty of Law, "Effectively, the red-light district had become a no-go area for the police."

In Amsterdam, the police "stole a march" on this effort by enforcing the new standards while the business was still *gedoogd,* modifying the existing rules to conform to the new law. Of course, tourists in *de Wallen* need not be concerned by the evolving situation; it is no more in the interests of the underworld to bother visitors than in those of the city as a whole.

In short, all the "sin" you see around you in *de Wallen* is a mix of legal and semilegal activity, all operating in a unique Dutch manner, according to *de regels.*

GROWING UP IN
DE WALLEN

Jules van Harn is a brash young man of twenty-five who was born
and raised in and around the Red-Light District. The son of a
Dutch journalist father and a French psychiatrist, Jules describes him-
self as a product of the "love generation." However, his father took a
leading role in the Nieuwmarkt riots of 1970s, when squatters, as-

sorted radicals, and ordinary Amsterdammers took violent exception to massive redevelopment to extend the metro system and permit heavy vehicular traffic access to the central station area. Battles raged in and about Nieuwmarkt, with the protesters going so far as to jury-rig two armor-plated cars, complete with pepper-firing cannon, to assault the police lines. These days of rage are, in unique Dutch style, commemorated today on the walls and floor of the Nieuwmarkt metro station, along with other notable events in the history of this square, on the border of the Red Light. For example, this beautiful square, today lined with lovely cafes and restaurants, was the fringe of the Old Jewish Quarter. During World War II, barbed wire surrounded de Waag as most of the city's large Jewish population, a vital part of Amsterdam's cultural and economic life since the fifteenth century, were deported to their deaths in Treblinka and Auschwitz.

Jules' formative years were spent in more peaceful times, largely living on Warmoesstraat, the street bordering the Red Light to the west. His were the days of the modern Red Light, not the grimmer, poorer, and often rowdier *Rosse Buurt,* which served mainly locals and seamen before the social turmoil of the late 1960s and 1970s—before the arrival of the age of mass air travel transformed the neighborhood forever. What was it like growing up in the middle of such a neighborhood?

As Jules remembers, he and his friends didn't take a lot of notice of the ladies in the windows until the age of eight or ten. Not surprising perhaps, except that, walking to school past the sex shops and porno shows of *de Wallen,* they were more exposed than most children to the explicit mechanics of sex. But Jules recalls the prostitutes as "just pretty ladies, not wearing much, of course." At his Catholic primary

Peep Show

Chickita's Sexshop

school, the teaching sisters showed no discrimination towards a schoolmate whose mother worked in a window, and he recalls no feeling of awkwardness when walking past her "work" area to the family living quarters upstairs.

As we spoke in the relaxed atmosphere of the Coffeeshop Betty Boop, which he manages, Jules expressed the near-nationalism of the native-born Amsterdammer, and a similar attachment to his native neighborhood. "I wouldn't live anywhere not near the Red Light," he contends, "and I won't raise my children in some boring suburb of Amsterdam." Where else could a young man get to know probably the oldest "working girl" in the neighborhood, rumored to be a still-active seventy-six years of age. Jules remembers hearing "Tante (Auntie) Anna," as we'll call her, apologize for missing a (nonprofessional) appointment because she'd had a new, young client who "took a long time."

There are negative memories as well. Passing the street junkies and derelicts in certain areas of the Red Light isn't a pleasant experience for adults today. For young Jules, the *tippelaars* were particularly scary. "I'd pass one on the way to school, and she'd pat me on the head and give me 25 cents, then look right through me a few hours later when she was flying." And some of his friends wound up directly or indirectly "in the life," one taking a prostitute as a steady girlfriend and another squandering his resources on what in America would be called a "sex addiction" to the windows.

Whether growing up in the environment of *de Wallen* is healthy or not is a question for armchair psychologists, moral philosophers, and professionals such as Jules' mother (who specializes in treating substance abuse). The presence of the many cannabis coffeeshops in the district would certainly be another factor to consider. Jules made his first illicit visit to a coffeeshop at twelve and remembers how upset his mother was a few years later, when she caught him smoking weed. In Amsterdam, trying marijuana is no different from underage drinking in other countries, to be actively discouraged, but no sure sign of a wasted life to follow. In fact, although Jules chose to work in the coffeeshop business, he gave up using his product several years ago, although not the Northern European affection for excessively alcoholic social occasions, arguably a worse vice. He spent three years at university before deciding on a career path which didn't require a degree. Healthy and happily married and working a stone's throw from *de Wallen*, he projects confidence that he will succeed, whatever his line of endeavor. And, don't forget, in Amsterdam a coffeeshop manager is not the evil "dope dealer" of countries with less-enlightened drug policies, but a responsible, taxpaying citizen engaged in a trade, which, although many Dutch disapprove, attracts millions of tourist dollars, and there's nothing more Dutch than that!

What is it like to raise a child in this environment? I was speaking to one acquaintance who raised two boys and had to pass the ladies in the windows with them daily when taking them to day care. She remembers when the younger child asked her what the women were doing standing there in their underwear. The older had already figured it out and rescued his mother, she thought, by self-importantly telling his brother, "They are selling love." Later, however, she was mortified to be asked, "Mommy, I don't have to pay you to love me, do I?" It was then she decided to move to another neighborhood.

THE LADIES IN THE WINDOWS

Prostitution exists in many forms and at many levels in Amsterdam. The form most tourists see is the ladies in the windows. At least a few of the more than 450 glass-door cubicles of the window brothels are staffed from late morning until the wee hours of the next day. The ladies, in their Frederick's of Hollywood best (and least) are a smorgasbord of women of all sizes, shapes, races, and nationalities. Few of them are Dutch. As the sex business exploded over the past quarter-century, most of the native-born ladies moved up from the windows to the new, upscale gentlemen's clubs outside the Red Light. At these elegant brothels, tourists and visiting businessmen can choose from an array of young women in the relaxed atmosphere of a comfortable cocktail lounge and spend from several hundred euros to a great deal more for an evening's entertainment. A visit to Amsterdam's five-star brothel, the Yab Yum, on the Singel can easily run to thousands.

The prostitutes of the window brothels these days come largely from the old Soviet bloc, the former Dutch colonies in Asia and the Caribbean, or impoverished areas in Latin America. As in every country's sex industry, there are those among them who are indentured servants (or, perhaps more accurately, "sex slaves"), coerced or tricked into coming, then presented with a bill—one that they can almost never repay—from their importers or the local entrepreneurs to whom they've been sold. But many arrive voluntarily, eyes wide open. In six months' to a year's hard work in the "cribs" of de Wallen, a woman from the impoverished East can earn enough to go back home, build a house, or open a small business.

The women are protected by Stichting de Rode Draad (the "hookers' union") which keeps them informed as to their tax and social insurance responsibilities, and makes financial planning advice available to members. The Dutch love woordspelingen (wordplay, puns), and I'm told the stichting took its name from the idea that prostitution is a "red thread" running through the fabric of human history.

Room to Rent

The basic charge for a fifteen-minute "trick" is €20—more for extra time or services, and much more for drunken disrespectful tourists. The industry is currently trying to get acceptance of €40 as the core price, as there hasn't been an increase in over twenty years, and recent changes in the law, discussed elsewhere, are causing increases in the cost of doing business. But, after paying €60–90 for a shift's rent of their work space (depending on location and time), even splitting out with a pimp or "boyfriend," a prostitute can make quite a good living in the windows.

NOT MY DAUGHTER?

When I decided to include a profile of an Amsterdam working girl in *Closed Curtain*, I was faced with a multiplicity of choices: *raamvrouw*; brothel prostitute; escort; or *tippelaar*. I was fortunate enough to meet a young lady with experience in all but the last subbranch of the trade. Although, as we'll see, Monique feels neither shame nor regret about her five and a half years "in the life," she still asked that I not use her real name.

We met, providentially enough, when I stopped in at the Prostitution Information Center on another matter. Monique had just begun to help out at the shop, and her articulate, outspoken attitudes led me to ask her to be our subject. Monique is a tall, matronly blonde in her mid-thirties, with a peaches-and-cream complexion and an authoritative attitude which would seem to suit her better to a classroom than a window.

Born into a typical Dutch middle-class family, Monique spent her first eleven years in Holland's second city of Rotterdam. Her father, a manager in the computer industry, then moved the family (wife, Monique, and her younger brother) to picturesque Haarlem, fifteen minutes from Amsterdam. Sex was never a taboo subject in the house; Monique remembers her mother being particularly frank and open. This, plus the normal sex education given Dutch children, and the existence of "window streets" in both Haarlem and Rotterdam, all fueled Monique's natural and healthy interest in "sexuality rather than just sex." Aware of some American bluenose and tabloid attitudes, Monique stresses that there was never a hint of sexual impropriety in her family life and, as for sex education in the schools, "educating people about sex doesn't mean they'll do it right away." Despite this early interest in matters sexual, including curiosity about prostitution, Monique did not become active herself until she was nineteen.

There are numerous factors which may lead a young woman into "the life." Many are the result of bad choices, while some may be beyond a girl's control: lack of education or job training; abusive/manipulative mates; drug addiction; or physical/economic coercion. In Monique's case, none of the above apply. In fact, if the title weren't already taken, I might have called this chapter "The Happy Hooker."

Her story may be atypically upbeat but is illustrative of some positives and negatives in Dutch policies and attitudes towards prostitution and affords a few insights into the workings of the business from a rank-and-file perspective.

Monique entered the "oldest profession" relatively late in life. After academic training in computers and personnel administration, she began her working life as an office worker and seemed destined for a respectable business career. Over the years, however, her interest in prostitution never diminished. "I really saw it as a way to help people and learn more about them," she says. She pestered her male acquaintances until they admitted "window-hopping" or brothel visits, then extracted details to find out what it was like to be a sex worker. She contemplated finding out firsthand for several years before she overcame the completely unfounded notion that she was too ugly to make a living "in the life." At the age of twenty-seven, when many working girls would be looking for a way out, Monique left the security and "boredom" of the straight world behind her to step instead into the realm of closed curtains. She made no secret of her choice to family, friends, or her work colleagues and swears that almost everyone, including her family, supported her in her decision (although I'd bet there were a few privately expressed reservations about her sanity).

With her old coworkers' best wishes for "good luck on the new job" ringing in her ears, and approval from both mother ("It's so exciting!") and father ("It's your life, live it for yourself."), Monique became part of the staff of one of Amsterdam's gentlemen's clubs. The job wasn't hard to find; most of the places listed in the Yellow Pages will try out any presentable applicant for what is a trial period for both the brothel and the prospective prostitute. Life as a "parlor girl" did not, however, turn out the way she'd imagined. "I thought the other girls would be supportive, show me the ropes. But they were cold and competitive. But when I entertained my first client, it felt like a homecoming. The place I worked also offered outcall service, and my first job was at a home for the elderly and disabled. He was a seventy-two-year-old man who was waiting for me with his zipper already undone. But, as we proceeded, it was obvious that the human contact meant more to him than the sex act."

After a few weeks, Monique decided that outcall escort work was more to her liking than competing for the attentions of any prospect who walked in the door. She spent the rest of her career as an escort, working on-call from her home, where a driver would pick her up and deliver her to the client's hotel, residence, or occasionally other "homes" such as the one at which she broke her professional maidenhead. In the escort trade, as in the brothels, the best way for prostitutes to maximize earnings is either to work longer hours and service more customers, or to sell more hours (extensions) to the clients they get. Monique enjoyed the work and, given her feeling that she should be bringing more than just fleeting physical release to her clientele, she was successful. Her one major complaint was over the financial "split" with the escort service. "They charged €115 an hour. I got €45, the driver €25, and the service €45. But that stayed the same even if I sold more hours, and if I did, the driver would go off-pay, so the service would make seventy! I know they pay for advertising and other expenses, but that doesn't seem at all fair to me!" (This sounds like one of the issues which will have to be addressed as the Netherlands continues to adjust to the October 2000 complete legalization of brothels and escort services.)

However, it was not the financial split that caused Monique to leave the agency. It is the dream of many, if not most, prostitutes that they will one day meet a client who will take her out of "the life" to a future of domestic bliss and respectability. Once in a while this happens. Although Monique wasn't necessarily looking to escape, she did meet someone and decided to leave the trade, hoping to pursue a university degree in counseling; she had already begun to do volunteer work at the Red Thread. As she thought she might like to work with sex workers as a counselor and might use her work experience as "field research" for course requirements, she decided that she would sample life on the next-to-bottom rung of the prostitution ladder. She spent a few days working in a window on the narrowest *raamstraat* ("window street") in *de Wallen*, around the corner from the Oude Kerk. This alleyway gets so crowded that the men have to walk sideways, back-to-back, and nose-to-nose with the ladies who, I'm told, do a high-volume business. Unfortunately, although Monique was willing to sit in a window, she couldn't bring herself to wear fluorescent undies and worked in a frock. Although she gathered research material, she didn't make a lot of money.

She also didn't make it to university; the relationship broke up before she started. Although she didn't want to go back to "the life," she still had a lot of compassion to share, so she got a job working for a *thuiszorg*, an organization providing light cleaning and companionship services to housebound senior citizens. She continued to take an interest in the welfare of her ex-colleagues while working part-time for a prostitutes' hotline which was featured on a television program. This brief glimpse of Monique was spotted by her employers, who unfortunately then let her go. "They were afraid I would be providing sexual services to the old people."

As of this writing, even in the very "liberal climate" of the Netherlands, Monique has found that a background in prostitution does not necessarily enhance one's employment history. Although her talents and experience make her a valuable addition to the Prostitution Information Center, it is a pity that society is being deprived of her drive, "people skills," and compassion in a broader capacity.

She has learned her lesson. "Don't use my name," she asked. "I like this job, but anything can happen, and you know how hard it can be to find new work."

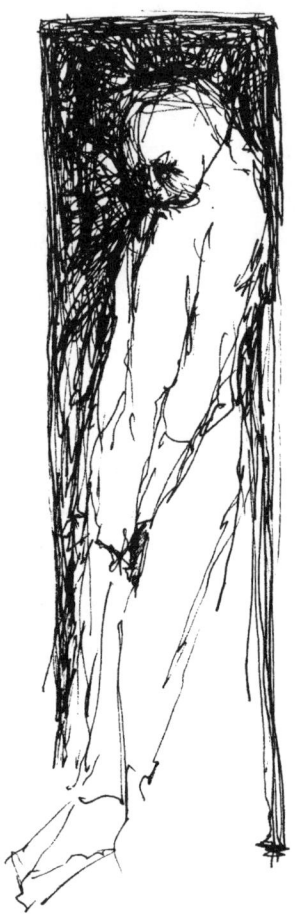

THE CLIENTELE

Who are the customers for the "horizontal trade?" Find a comfortable spot with a view of a bank of *Wallen* windows and perch for a while, and you'll see a cross-section of the male population window-shopping and popping in and out of the doorways for their quarter-hour clinical sexual experience. Suited businessmen, workmen in leather jackets, sailors, students, tourists, any man, it seems, may succumb to an "impulse purchase" in this supermarket of sex.

Many of the women have their own regular clients, once or twice a week visitors drawn by physical attributes or skill in particular sex acts. For men who, for whatever reason, are not married or in a relationship, time spent with an attractive lady in an intimate setting can provide therapeutic emotional and physical release. Many men also have exotic fantasies they are unable or unwilling to ask their regular part-

ners to fulfill. And, as one acquaintance who is a window brothel regular remarks, "Where else can you walk down the street and find the spitting image of an old, lost love, or the girl who shot you down in high school, on display and available for a few moments of fantasy?"

As you walk through *de Wallen*, you'll see that there are ladies to satisfy any taste. There are streets where most women are African, along others Asians predominate, yet others feature mainly Europeans. There are hefty women and *Playboy* centerfolds, old and young. S&M fetishists will even find dominatrices summoning them from windows advertising their specialty.

ETIQUETTE

If you're a single man strolling past the windows and slow down to enjoy the scenery, you'll likely find yourself the object of finger-tapping on the glass or inviting words whispered from cracked doorways. Just shake your head and walk on, and you won't be further accosted. But, if you stand too long or start to negotiate, and then walk by, you may find yourself being loudly described to the whole street in language which, if you're lucky, you won't understand. Stop to take an

The Condomerie

unauthorized snapshot, and you'll quickly find out that, in addition to their "union," the prostitutes of de Wallen also have their own "protectors" lounging unobtrusively nearby. And if clients get out of line, each room is equipped with a red button to summon help. If you want to window-shop without buying, at least have the courtesy not to gape oafishly, laugh hysterically, or point women out to your friends for comment—behavior all too common among our more inebriated visitors. Please bear in mind that Wallen women work hard and are as deserving of respect as any other service professionals.

Although there are no legal requirements or inspections to ensure that prostitutes practice safe sex, generally no prostitute in de Wallen will entertain a client without a condom. On that subject, any visit to the district should include a stop at the Condomerie. This delightful shop on Warmoesstraat was founded in 1987 in response to the growing AIDS epidemic. Just as the Prostitution Information Center allows you to have your questions answered without embarrassment, at the Condomerie, you can find publications on safe sex, receive advice on the right condom for you (or your partner), and delight over a vast selection of condoms of all sizes and whimsical designs, along with other "fun fantasy" creations.

TIPPELAARS

We mentioned that it is possible for some sex workers in the window brothels to graduate to employment in one of the posher sex clubs in town. There is also a step down on the prostitution career ladder, from which it is difficult to climb back up. *Tippelaars* are streetwalkers who specialize in providing furtive satisfaction to their customers in automobiles, alleyways, or anywhere with a hint of semi-privacy. "Curb crawling" is not illegal for the women or

their clients, but their activities can cause obvious problems in the narrow, crowded streets of de Wallen. Several years ago, Amsterdam opened an official tippelzone for streetwalkers. You are unlikely to stumble across this area on your own. It is located near the western docks, a good twenty-minute drive from the city center. And drive you must; there is no public transportation nearby, and pedestrian shoppers are rare.

The tippelzone is open daily from 9 p.m. until 3 a.m. and occupies a specially built, gated side street. Every night, the cars of the first of hundreds of customers are lined up bumper to bumper outside, waiting to inspect the 80-130 prostitutes on display. Many tippelaars are drug addicts, and bargaining is routine, with prices in the €12-17 range. But if a woman (or man; many streetwalkers are "pre-op" transsexuals or transvestites) is desperate enough, the price may be driven down further still, a prostitute persuaded to engage in unprotected sex, or, equally dangerous, leave the security of the zone in a client's car.

You'll see all sorts of vehicles turning into the tippelzone, from luxury sedans to the occasional bicycle as a seaman pedals from his ship to take his pleasure standing against the wall of one of the afwerkplekken (climax places; literally, "finishing off places"). These are tilt-up concrete enclosures in a row, much like California carports, fully equipped with waste disposal containers. The afwerkplek is in some respects a type of drive-through service. The government health authorities operate a shelter in the zone, dispensing free condoms and coffee, and providing a place for the workers to get off their feet (or knees) and out of the weather for a few minutes.

It's not a great life for most *tippelaars*, and it's not surprising that they are the victims of a great deal of violence, even murder. Their vulnerability puts them at the mercy of "control freaks" and the occasional psychopath among their clientele. However, as a social control, the *tippelzones* (they exist in other cities throughout the country) perform several useful functions, providing some security for the prostitutes, making them readily accessible to their customers, and keeping them, by and large, from the streets of residential neighborhoods. You may still encounter *tippelaars* in *de Wallen* or congregating behind the central station; many are illegals avoiding the regulation of the zone, while others are junkies who do not want to be too far from their drug connections.

Since it's hard to be upbeat about *tippelaars'* lives, I might as well go all the way to pure schmalz and close with a haunting image given me by one of my sources. Just as the *tippelzone* is only accessible to customers by means of some sort of transportation, so do the workers need a vehicle, or a friend with one, to get to and from work. Otherwise, it's a €25 taxi ride, not much of an affordable option on the best night at their rates, or face the long walk to Sloterdijk, the nearest metro station. In the predawn grayness, it is not unusual to see groups of weary, stranded streetwalkers converging on the station, where there will still be a wait for the day's first trains. Of course, there's always the chance of conducting some end-of-shift business on the platform! One *tippelaar* interviewed in a Dutch magazine works exclusively on the commuter trains from Amsterdam west, meeting new and regular "tricks" on board, and servicing them at the other end, going back and forth like a yo-yo for four hours a day.

TOP OF THE LADDER: YAB YUM

There have always been distinct classes of whoredom. In ancient Athens, the portside bawds of Piraeus were a far cry from the sophisticated *heterae*, high-priced courtesans whose salons were frequented by lawmakers and philosophers as much for the conversation as for more physical entertainment, for which they were also likely to turn to young (male) protégés. The present-day counterparts of the *heterae* may be found in exclusive men's clubs around the world. We've already discussed the bottom rung of the prostitution career ladder (*tippelaars*) and the next rung, the *raamvrouwen* (window ladies). We'll conclude our look at the ladies with a visit to Amsterdam's five-star brothel: Yab Yum.

There are twenty pages of "escort services" listed in the Amsterdam Yellow Pages (only in Las Vegas have I seen more). Many of these are outcall establishments, dispatching women (and men) to their clients' hotels. There are among them a dozen or so which offer, on their own premises, a more complete entertainment experience than just a little "slap and tickle." A few years ago, in my lifelong quixotic quest for outrageous (and legitimate) tax deductions, I visited one of them, to be nameless here, in researching an article for an American magazine. At the time, I was quite impressed by the genteel Victorian cocktail lounge and the easy hospitality of the "hostess," who greeted clients and effected introductions to a selection of lovely, well-dressed young women. The entry cost was €30, which covered two drinks at the bar ("But it's best not to have both before," advised the hostess.). This was applied to the first hour you spent in one of the rooms. The cost of a lady and a room was €230, and the décor of the rooms was reminiscent of tacky "adult" motels in the United States.

Yab Yum, which doesn't advertise in the telephone book and is unlisted in the regular directory, offers a different experience. The club relies on word of mouth, distribution of brochures to patrons, and its website (www.yabyum.com). The taxi drivers of Amsterdam, as in other cities, are willing sources of information and recommendations on erotic venues. They receive a commission on referrals and, unlike elsewhere, don't have to worry about being harassed or arrested, and their fares don't have to worry about being steered to some low dive (unless that's what they're looking for). For *Closed Curtain*, of course, we didn't want to report on less than the top of the line, but our research budget was limited, and we'd heard that it would cost a bit more than €30 to gain entry to a bordello which modestly bills itself as "the most exclusive and pleasant men's club in the world." Fortunately, I had made the acquaintance of Xaviera Hollander, the original "Happy Hooker." As a horny adolescent in the States in the mid-1960s when the sexual revolution was in its infancy, I—like millions of my peers—was amazed and delighted when this young Dutch woman was arrested for running an elite call-girl operation from a luxury Manhattan apartment. Instead of accepting shame and scandal, she used her notoriety to speak out against the hypocrisy of a "free" country which forced working women into the criminal classes and fostered corruption on a massive scale among the civil servants, police officers, prosecutors, and judges who were charged with enforcing an unenforceable law, and who were as likely to turn up in a hooker's "trick book" as anyone else. Her testimony before the Knapp Commission investigating police corruption was sensational, as was the icy allure of her classic Dutch good looks, short blonde hair framing her high cheekbones, and penetrating blue eyes. Xaviera was always impeccably turned out as well as outspoken. Although her activities in the United States made her persona non grata there, as a true daughter of a great nation of traders, she parlayed her celebrity into literary success with *The Happy Hooker* and, at last count, sixteen subsequent volumes of memoirs and advice, a long-running column in *Penthouse* magazine, and, today, proprietorship of a bed and breakfast inn and dinner theater ("The Happy Booker"), both operated from her classic home in one of Amsterdam's best neighborhoods (www.xaviera.com). It had been a pleasure to finally meet this sexual icon (who has weathered the intervening years considerably better than your humble narrator) of my youth, and she was gracious enough to help arrange a strictly journalistic visit to Yab Yum for Michelle and myself.

Yab Yum occupies a stately four-story brick building on the Singel canal, a few blocks west of the Royal Palace. An oversized green lantern beckons invitingly over the carved oak doors, which are capped by a relief of the club's logo of two doves smooching in front of a red heart. A tuxedoed doorman ushered us into the reception area, where we saw a long marble coat-check desk, matching green wall panels adorned with gilt-framed oils. Gilded Buddhas behind and upon the counter, and the greenish tint of the fixtures proved a foretaste of broad themes continued in the private rooms upstairs. Tapering chandeliers, like stalactites of glowing ice, illuminated the area.

The lady we were to meet was busy when we arrived, so a sterling silver coffee service was laid before us in the bar, and, as the club had just opened (hours are from 8 p.m. to 4 a.m. daily), we were left alone to wait and absorb the ambiance of the room, as the barman prepared for the evening's onslaught. We were seated in a lounge area furnished with plush white divans and marble-topped cocktail tables. This occupied one-third of the approximately 1,500 square feet. The other end houses the marble-topped oval bar, from behind which, against the far wall, Buddha beams over the room, flanked by tasteful etched-glass nudes. Between the bar and lounge, there is a small dance floor, flanked by stools and high tables. A narrow, gilded wooden balcony projects over the lounge area, housing amplifiers and a deejay station.

The room would be comfortably full with fifty people, although, as the club entertains an average of thirty customers nightly, they'd all

have to be there at once, with a corresponding number of ladies, for it to fill up. In the wee hours, however, as satisfied clients come down from the boudoirs and are free, having spent freely, to relax post-coitus at the bar or work out the last of their energies on the dance floor on the way out, the nightclub aspect of Yab Yum can become quite lively.

Although the designer of Yab Yum chose an eclectic mix of styles in decorating this pleasure place, to me the overall effect in the bar seems tilted toward Second French Empire, perhaps suggested by the painted ceiling depicting blue skies, clouds, and framing greenery, which seems to open up the room almost like a skylight.

After a few moments, we were approached by a slim, well-dressed young woman, who looked to Michelle "like a typical attractive Dutch college girl." As mentioned elsewhere, although prostitution and brothel-keeping are legal, there is still a social stigma attached to the business among the rest of a people still strongly influenced by Calvinist roots, so most of those "in the life" do not want to advertise the fact. My first glimpse of our interviewee, her aplomb and form, reminded me of a young Audrey Hepburn, so we'll call her that.

Yab Yum, like the modern Red-Light District, dates from the mid-1970s. Audrey had been working there for over two years and held the position of "coordinator" between the management of the club itself, and the fifty or so women who work there as independent subcontractors. This position entails interviewing and hiring the young ladies, making sure that they meet not only high standards of physical beauty, but are also able to elevate the customer's experience from a tawdry bit of groping to a higher social and esthetic level. Obviously, no customer of the window brothels of de Wallen is likely to buy a €1,150 bottle of champagne for a lady he met when she tapped her keys on the glass at him, or to buy more time than required to satisfy his basic physical needs and desires. At Yab Yum, most girls only entertain on average one client a night, and they only make real money when they can successfully "suggest" a bottle or two of bubbly, on which they earn a commission, and/or provide such irresistible company that the customer extends his stay for a second hour, a third, and beyond. Only 20–30 percent of Yam Yum's clientele are Dutch. The majority of the balance are visiting businessmen, willing to spend for value received. But, as a three-hour session with wine and snacks can easily put €7,000 or more on a patron's credit card or expense account, the women must obviously offer not only impressive sexual skills, but social ones as well. "They have to be able to talk," Audrey said, "and to keep up on current events. If a client is upset about the Dow Jones, he expects the girl to at least know what he's talking about."

When asked why most women apply for jobs at the club, Audrey's reply was simple: big money. Since many of the girls are new to "the life" (including college students, bored housewives, and other part-timers), part of Audrey's job is to make sure they know what they're getting into. "I explain that the money is very good, but that the work is very hard, and that they will not want to do it for more than two or three years. I tell them it is important to start a savings or investment program from the very beginning, so that they will have a nest egg when they decide to move on to something else."

I'd heard that an evening's entertainment at Yab Yum generally couldn't be had for less than €1,000. This proved to be a conservative estimate. It can be done, but only for what would be a definitely barebones experience. While waiting for Audrey, we looked over the bar menu. This featured Sevruga Caviar (€205), Garnished Smoked

Salmon (€115), and Goose-liver Pate (€115). To wash down such gourmet fare, what else but a selection of fine champagnes, ranging in price from €250 to €800. For those committed to only the best, there were also magnums of Taittinger Millennium, from an exclusive Yab Yum bottling of 1,000, priced at a modest €1,150. Our next questions were, therefore, naturally channeled toward the cost of services.

It costs €75 to gain entrance to the club. This entitles patrons to complementary drinks (except champagne) in the bar while examining the ladies on display. The entrance charge is in addition to the base price of €450 for services in the private rooms. This covers not only the lady (or ladies, although double the fun is twice the price) involved but pays for the facility, its staff of seventeen, and the security and promotional services provided by the management (including, I'm sure, a more-than-handsome profit). If a patron hangs about in the bar for an hour without becoming an upstairs client, he, she or they (women and couples are welcome) will be politely asked to select a companion or leave.

If a customer at the bar is interested in meeting a lady, he (or as above) need only mention it to the bartender, who will effect an introduction. If the girl is suitable, the couple will move, as Michelle, Audrey, and I did (again, I regret to say, with purely journalistic and artistic intent), to one of the eleven private rooms.

If the rooms at the club I had visited earlier reminded me of an American XXX "no tell" motel, those at Yab Yum were more like those one would find at a posh honeymoon resort. The rooms are equipped with large circular beds, the upholstered headboards topped by gilded wood sculptures of languidly reclining nudes, small divans, and other elegant incidental furniture. Lighting is indirect, and the recurrent

color schemes of gold and green (with some red, of course) and the eclectic mix of decorating styles, continue in the boudoirs. Porcelain Indian elephants with howdahs serve as drink platforms, and abstract metal coat racks sport conical green breasts. Nudes in the Italian Classic Revival style vie, but do not clash with erotic artwork with Turkish or French influences, and just a touch of Art Deco. Music or erotic videos are available, and room service to keep the champagne bucket full, or cater to other client whims, is always available. The amenities provided rival those of any five-star hotel: terry-cloth robes and slippers; loofahs; dental floss, toothpaste, and toothbrushes; combs; breath spray; bubble bath; and, of course, condoms.

Although many of the other clubs in Amsterdam advertise orgy rooms, S&M dungeons, and other attractions for fetishists, the only concession to the unconventional at Yab Yum is the "party room," essentially the same as the other bedrooms, but furnished with two huge beds, easily roomy enough to accommodate a half-dozen revellers and their companions. If handcuffs, whips and chains, or other sex toys are required, room service, again, is always available to bring them.

The brothel's glossy, illustrated brochure claims that "A visit to Yab Yum could very well be the highlight of your stay in Amsterdam" and that "Some nights just never end." The club's 4 a.m. closing time need not signal the end of the night's pleasure. Patrons are free to make arrangements with the management to take one or more of the ladies out for early morning revelry at their hotels or at other entertainment spots. The same cabdriver grapevine which brings many customers to Yab Yum also serves as an informal security system for women continuing the night on outcall.

A few nights after Michelle and I made our visit, I went back to Yab Yum with a young American friend to get a little more information for our readers. The bar was just beginning to get busy, with four or five customers, and about the same number of elegant, alluring young ladies on display. While I asked my questions, my friend sipped a beer and seemed oddly subdued. When we left, I asked what he thought of the talent on display. "I couldn't look," he said, shamefaced. "I knew if I did, I'd be lost. Do you know where I can get €500 for my car at this hour?"

PROSTITUTION IS A JOB!

Across from the Oude Kerk, in the heart of *de Wallen*, you'll come across an institution unique to Amsterdam. Right next door to an agency renting rooms in window brothels, the Prostitution Information Center is an interesting and entertaining source of material on the "oldest" profession. The P.I.C. is the brainchild of Mariska Majoor, herself a veteran of five years "in the life." After leaving the trade, she began publishing a quarterly *Pleasure Guide*, then broke into the public

eye big-time in July 1994, when she organized the Prostitution Mani-
festation in Dam Square, a huge celebration of the rights of working
girls to be treated with dignity and respect. Following the success of
this event, Majoor opened the P.I.C. a month later.

The P.I.C. is a nonprofit foundation devoted to educating the
public on the sex trade and fostering acceptance of prostitution as a
respected profession, to be regulated like any other. Enter the inviting
storefront headquarters, and you're confronted with an array of books
and magazines, in Dutch and English, all about the sex business in Amsterdam, the rest of the Netherlands, and around the world. These include *Black Light*, published by de Rode Draad and *Danzine*, a lively
American quarterly. Mariska's own publications are on sale, including
her latest, *Als sex werken wordt* (*When Sex Becomes Work*), a detailed
explanation of the workings of the industry written for men and
women who plan to become prostitutes.

In addition to publications, the P.I.C. handles a wide range of
Red-Light souvenirs, including a one-page map of the area's brothel
streets (drawn by Mariska's father, Jaap Majoor, whose prints of neighborhood scenes also adorn the walls), T-shirts, postcards, and erotic
novelties. There is even a replica of a typical window brothel room,
where you can have your picture taken for the folks back home (although a live hostess or gigolo is not provided).

The P.I.C. is not geared just to curious tourists, but is also a re-
source for the working girls of *de Wallen* and for their clients. One
P.I.C. product takes a whimsical spin on the Dutch obsession with *de
regels*. As I glanced at the list of "Rules for Clients," I noticed one in
particular: "Keep your body fresh!" I commented that I'd always
thought one of the worst parts of a prostitute's job would be dealing

Behind a Closed Curtain

with customers who are strangers to personal hygiene. Mariska's raised eyebrows and vehement "You've got that right!" told me I'd awakened unpleasant olfactory memories.

If you're curious about the Red Light, interested in working there, or planning to become more than just a window-shopper, Mariska will be glad to provide you with any information you require, without fear of embarrassment. She also is available to address groups. When I stopped in one day, she was making a presentation to a class of Belgian students in their early teens. Advice is free, but if you don't make a purchase, a donation to help the P.I.C. in its mission is required.

THE WHORES' UNION

Although it is popular to refer to Stichting de Rode Draad as a hookers' union, it is not a labor organization and has no membership roles. The Red Thread represents "working girls" only as an advocate of prostitutes' rights and as a source of information and support for sex workers in the Netherlands. It has its roots in the world-wide surge of feminist activism of the 1970s and 1980s. The Dutch government had already established the Mr A. de Graaf Stichting to study and make recommendations on issues of prostitution. Although de Graaf is dedicated to changing the image of the oldest profession from despicable to respectable, it is essentially a think tank. When women seeking help and advice turned to them, staffers felt helpless, able only to provide informal advice and facilities for meetings. Advocacy and outreach were outside de Graaf's official brief and beyond the resources of its state budget. A more direct approach was obviously needed. Advice from de Graaf, pressure from sex workers, and the unconditional support of Dutch feminists led to the opening of the Red Thread in 1985.

This is not the first time that the feminist agenda has enfolded issues of prostitution. During the struggle for female suffrage in the United States, a prominent activist was Victoria C. Woodhull, a one-time traveling clairvoyant who achieved success on Wall Street after becoming "spirit" consultant to Commodore Cornelius Vanderbilt. She operated the first female-owned brokerage firm on the Street and published a successful newspaper, while becoming a spokeswoman for female rights, sharing the stage at rallies with Susan B. Anthony and Elizabeth Cady Stanton. In 1872, nearly forty years before she and her sisters won the right to vote, she became the first woman to run for the presidency of the United States. The platform of her Equal Rights Party called for full civil rights for women, including control of their own property and their bodies, even if they chose to sell them. Neither the male hierarchy nor her sister feminists were ready for Woodhull's "free love" message, for her own flexible marital arrangements, or for the rumors that, in her early career, she had assisted her clients with more tangible benefits than a glimpse into the next world. While Ms. Anthony went on to great fame, lived to an honored old age, and was briefly memorialized on her country's coinage, Woodhull died in obscurity and exile in England.

The alliance between feminism and prostitution was broken for almost a century, until the next great wave of women's activism. The renewed relationship resulted in the establishment in the United States, in the mid-1960s, of COYOTE ("Call Off Your Old Tired Ethics"). This group was founded by Margo St. James, a former prostitute in North Beach, San Francisco's version of de Wallen. COYOTE and other sex workers' groups are still active in America, but have had their greatest successes in improving conditions in legal strip clubs and lap-dancing parlors—except for parts of Nevada, prostitution remains illegal everywhere in the USA. Only in the Netherlands is the government an active participant in the protection of prostitutes' rights.

The offices of de Rode Draad are in a canal house a few blocks from the Red Light. A little threadbare and in need of dusting, they resemble an underfunded political campaign headquarters, with scattered metal desks strewn with file folders and piles of literature. Interim Director Jan Visser, a veteran of over twenty years with de Graaf Foundation, discussed the Red Thread with me.

Red Thread's mission is to actively promote prostitutes' civil and social rights and to inform sex workers of them. Since its establishment, the organization has been instrumental in the extension of Dutch social welfare benefits and public health safety nets to prostitutes. Ongoing activities include referrals to legal and financial advisors, provision of facilities for group encounter and planning meetings, and lobbying for any change in law or public policy which will improve the status and welfare of its constituency. The foundation also maintains a media presence aimed at improving public perception of the sex industry.

At the time of my visit, the Dutch government had only recently legalized adult sex businesses. A major concern of Visser and de Rode Draad is making sure that sex workers are aware of their new status, and in advising on problem areas which have arisen in the process of implementation of the law. These include redefining the legal relationship between brothel-keepers and prostitutes in order to make most regular employees rather than shift-workers who, in some clubs must pay for the right to work. As more prostitutes operate in complete legality, banks, which have traditionally refused to open business accounts for sex workers, must be persuaded to change their policies. Guidelines must also be developed for local authorities to deal with applications for brothel licenses. The new law does not permit denial of a license on moral grounds, but does allow each jurisdiction substantial leeway in limiting the number, location, appearance, and size of sex businesses. Visser feels that legalization will eventually provide a "precise instrument" for regulation of brothels and protection of their employees, which was missing under the previous policy of "regulated tolerance."

I asked Visser how many prostitutes are working in Amsterdam, a number I've seen estimated to be anywhere from several to many thousands. His best guess, which is as authoritative as any, is "about 2,000." A real count is difficult. Official data is incomplete, many immigrants are illegally employed "in the life," and *tippelaars* often work "black" (with unreported income). The extent of sex slavery is also difficult to assess. Although tightening of regulation has made it almost impossible for illegals to find work in the windows, and legalization of other sex businesses will bring their employees under improved government oversight, there are, and will continue to be illegal sex clubs and brothels which provide a market for traffickers in women who are imported through deceit and kept by combinations of blackmail, fear, and coercion. Many involuntary prostitutes may also be working in brothels in the close-knit communities of North and West African immigrants in the southeastern outskirts of the city, where police penetration is problematical.

Among the handouts I collected at the Red Thread was one which listed "Rights of a Prostitute." As I looked them over, it occurred to me that, stripped of the unique trappings of the trade, the following is a list of basic human rights, even if the Netherlands is the only country to extend them to the oldest profession:

- You have the right to a safe and hygienic environment.
- You always have the right to refuse a client.
- You also have the right to refuse certain sexual acts.
- You may not be forced to drink alcohol or use drugs.
- You have the right to decide when you stop working.
- You may not be forced to work without condoms.
- You have the right to decide when and which doctor you want to see. The results of the test are confidential.

Here's a final observation, and a question for the Dutch government: If we accept a figure of 2,000 prostitutes for Amsterdam, a city of some 800,000, then these working girls and boys represent 0.25 percent of the population. Even if the concentration in the capital is twice that of the rest of the country, out of 16 million people, there would be about 25,000 men and women plying the trade in the Netherlands. When you consider all the other people in the sex trade, owners and employees, whose livelihood is based on the backbreaking (pun intended) labor of those 25,000 souls, and the enormous revenues they generate (and mostly pay taxes on), surely prostitutes are a constituency and a source of economic benefit worth protecting. Wouldn't it be reasonable for the Public Health Ministry, which funds the Red Thread, to come up with a few more euros for its budget, which was, as of this writing, just large enough to provide 3–4 part-time workers to fulfill an important and delicate mission?

GAY AMSTERDAM

In writing about gay life in *de Wallen* and other areas of Amsterdam, I was challenged to produce a piece which would be interesting and informative to both our "straight" visitors (without offending them) and to our many thousands of "pink" tourists (without boring them). Gay tourists—some estimates put them at 25 percent of the total—tend to visit Amsterdam to openly practice and celebrate a lifestyle which is still prosecuted and persecuted in many areas of the world. I knew I'd lose the outright homophobes with the chapter title. But I still had to hold our imaginary Aunt Tillie, her (also fictional) gay "in the closet" nephew Jack the accountant, and everyone in between. Back home in Tulsa, Jack is just another "suit." But as Tillie unpacks her flannels at one of Amsterdam's Golden Tulip hotels, Jack is hanging up his CPA's three-piece in favor of full-leather gear, complete with hood and strategically placed zippers, having checked into the master/slave suite at the Black Tulip. This, the city's premiere leather hotel, features S&M paraphernalia in every room, the perfect base for Jack's annual metamorphosis to "Master Jacques" and his nightly prowls through Gaydam. What could I put out that would be fresh and informative for such a wide range of readership?

A Little History

In the Netherlands, the emergence of a gay lifestyle from the shadows was a much more pacific process than in other countries. Homosexuality has not been prosecuted here since the nineteenth century, but until the period between the world wars, it was still, as the Victorians put it, "the love that dares not speak its name." In the 1920s and 1930s, there was a brief period of sunshine for European gays (remember *Cabaret*?), which extended to Amsterdam where several homo-venues flourished. Bet van Beeren, the original "Dyke on a Bike," opened the first gay women's bar here in 1927. But the Nazi occupation, which targeted homosexuals as well as Jews and Gypsies for extinction, was a tragic setback. Present-day visitors will find the Homo Monument, three pink granite triangles set in a triangle (representing the patches worn by gay concentration camp inmates), right in front of the Westerkerk, just steps from the Anne Frank House.

Gay Amsterdam bounced back quickly from the dark wartime period. The world's first openly homosexual affinity group was founded here in 1946, at first called the Shakespeare Club, then later the Cultuur- en Ontspanningscentrum (Culture and Leisure Center). While this discreet title provided a seemingly innocent front for gay dances and meetings, the acronym COC hinted at its orientation. The COC's activities were at first overseen by the Amsterdam Zeden-politie (Vice Squad). By 1955, the first gay-friendly hotels had opened, and a sprinkling of bars and clubs had sprung up around the Amstel and Rembrandtsplein areas, a short distance from the Red Light. In *de Wallen* proper, homoerotic entertainment venues were then, as now, centered on Warmoesstraat. And, as now, the dominant culture in the bars and clubs was leather-loving "rough trade."

While the rest of *de Wallen* went from gritty to glitzy, its homosexual attractions continued, as always, to range from the cozy to the raunchily outrageous. But Master Jacques and his friends had been escaping to Gaydam to "breathe free" and act out openly for years before the 1969 Stonewall Rebellion kicked off the gay liberation movement in the United States.

Gaydam Today

As I've mentioned, the leather scene is concentrated in the Red Light, but there are other gay attractions all over town. GayMap Amsterdam, freely available at most homo-oriented businesses, shows 108 exclusively gay or gay-friendly shops, hotels, sex saunas, bars, clubs, and brothels in the city center. Although *Closed Curtain* is the only English-language publication available for the general public on "vice" in the Red Light and elsewhere in Amsterdam, there are a number of more targeted free magazines and maps available for our "pink" visitors, several commercial periodicals sold at newsstands, and a number of gay-specific guidebooks in print. There is even a Pink Point of Presence gay information center (open May–August) located in front of the Homo Monument.

Almost every visitor to Amsterdam strolls through the cafe-lined Rembrandtsplein and nearby attractions, including the adjacent Thorbeckeplein and the world-famous canal-side *bloemenmarkt* (flower market). During the day, unless you stop in at one of the businesses flying the six-striped gay Rainbow Flag, you may be unaware that this is also one of the centers of homosexual life in the city center. In addition to the street artists, "straight" pubs, casinos, nightclubs, and eating places, this area is home to Gaydam's premiere gay male disco (It) and its only lesbian dance club (You II) as well as a selection of hustler bars doing nighttime trade, homo brown bars, and spots catering to drag queens.

Along nearby Reguliersdwarsstraat, which runs parallel to and east of the flower market, you'll also find a cluster of gay-friendly shops, bars, and restaurants, which, again, many hetero tourists would not recognize as such, although the Stringslip underwear shop might give a hint. If you walk south on Leidsestraat from the flower market towards the coffeeshops, cafes, and music clubs around Leidseplein, you pass Kerkstraat. This street boasts another collection of rainbow-bannered attractions, running several blocks on either side of Leidsestraat, including several hotels, as well as a fitness center and the Thermos Night Sauna. Gaydam offers a number of gay *sekssaunas* (including the Thermos Day), where the guys can get pretty frisky. My "inside" man tells me that the Thermos Night's action includes "unspeakable" acts. I didn't ask for more detail.

I was able to augment the gleanings of my own forays into the clubs and shops of Warmoesstraat with input from a San Francisco man who is a regular visitor to Gaydam. His description of the appeal of the fabled narrow lane to "pink" visitors is certainly as good, and more authoritative, than any I could write. "The tawdry, steamy, openly sexual atmosphere appeals to the typical repressed homosexual tourists, most of whom come from places where the sight of a dildo in a shop window would cause panic in the streets." This statement also applies to the fascination of many hetero visitors to the "straight" attractions of the Red Light.

Gay visitors tend to be more participatory than other tourists, and Warmoesstraat is "the strip" for the city's leather scene. "Rough trade" and "leather boys/men" make up perhaps the most extreme group among male homosexual fetishists—and the most prone to certain extreme, sometimes dangerous sexual practices. "Tops" and "bottoms" (not design coordinates!) congregate in full regalia, or close to none, nightly at the Cockring disco and the four other leather bars along the street, drinking, dancing, ingesting "tolerated" and illegal substances, and perhaps slipping into the "darkroom" for some semi-public, often anonymous satisfaction. The clubs are open from 11 p.m. to 4 a.m. (5 a.m. on weekends).

Bars with "darkrooms" (or dungeons!) all post prominent signs stating that "only safe sex will be tolerated on the premises," and condoms are freely available to all, but my informant notes that these "grope rooms" still attract a lot of gamblers. These clubs also feature products and amenities you won't find in most public, licensed premises. "Poppers" (vials of the heart stimulant amyl nitrite) are sniffed to enhance orgasmic intensity, while shots of nitrous oxide may be inhaled to heighten the hilarity of dancing or other activity. At the

Stablemaster, which hosts "sex parties" four nights a week in its tiny bar (not the upstairs "darkroom"), there are jars of Wetshaft water-based lubricant lined up along the bar like ketchup bottles at a diner. I stopped in one afternoon at a time when the bar is closed and doubles as reception for the homo-hotel upstairs. The stablemaster on duty proudly informed me that the "J.O." (jack-off) party record was eighty-

Lube Center

four celebrants, sweaty, male bodies writhing against one another in a room which would be comfortably full with twenty patrons.

Although the leather scene dominates the gay Red Light, such clubs as Dirty Dick's ("The Sleaze Pit") and Club Jacques (no relation) hardly stand out during the day. I've often seen "straight" tourists, almost always women, posing for photographs under the graphic Cockring logo, without a clue as to what would be going on inside later on. Only the most adventurous hetero male would venture into these clubs during peak hours (women are not allowed in any of them). But there are plenty of other opportunities for glimpses at Amsterdam's gay face along Warmoesstraat. There are shops offering tattoos and piercing (scrotum: €70; "Prince Albert": €95), shops selling leather, rubber, twisted gear, and gay porn, often all under the same roof. Speaking of smut, the Adonis Cinema and Sex Shop may be de Wallen's only exclusively gay porno palace, but if you step into any of the others in the neighborhood, you'll find that Amsterdam's "straight" sex shops are, in fact, omnisexual, catering to hetero and homosexual fantasies, as well as to fans of bestiality and other unmentionable preferences (yes, Tillie, even worse. Ask Jacques.).

There are several other gay-friendly (but not leather) bars along Warmoesstraat, where women are welcome if they don't gape and gasp. The Casa Maria, for example, is a cozy saloon about midway down the street, an excellent spot to relax with a cocktail and watch the passing parade. Right across the street is Getto, one of Gaydam's favorite restaurants, also with a good view of the street. What's that, Tillie? What's a "gay" restaurant? Well, it obviously has more to do with ownership, attitude, and atmosphere than the food, although the cocktails at happy hour do tend toward the "froufrou" variety. It's also a place where Master Jacques, in full regalia, can take Aunt Tillie for a

Dirty Dick's

Mr. B's Body Art Emporium

Quick Refueling

meal and some entertainment without attracting unwelcome attention (unless Tillie is impolite enough to giggle at the drag queens at the next table.) For hetero visitors who want to observe but not mingle, you can take window seats at a number of "straight" Warmoesstraat bars and coffeeshops.

At the risk of offending our Sapphic visitors, and possibly Aunt Tillie, I'll contend that female homosexuals have historically benefitted from a male-dominated society which condemns all same-sex physical love, but feels less threatened by woman-to-woman affection. Although outrageously "butch" appearance or behavior might cause a woman or a couple problems, discreet relationships among females were traditionally ignored, even tolerated.

Whether due to this ease of assimilation into the hetero world, the pressure on women to marry and bear children, the inferior social status of women, or a combination of factors, lesbians have always been a minority among overt homosexuals. Although the feminist and gay liberation movements helped many women "come out," this remains true today, even in Amsterdam. This does not mean that gay women have no reason to come to Amsterdam. Although there is only one exclusively women's bar (You II), there are plenty of lesbian-friendly dances and other social activities available, as well as *vrouwencafés* (women's cafes) such as Sarrein on the Elandstraat, Café Van den Berg on the Lindengracht, and Same Place on the Nassaukade. Among the gay city guides, you can look for *Dykes Below Sea Level*, which not only profiles the bar, club, and sex scenes, but is full of more general cultural and tourist info from a lesbian perspective. Amsterdam COC hosts many events for homosexuals of all ages and persuasions.

Since its founding in 1946, the Cultuur- en Ontspanningscentrum has evolved along with the community it serves. Although its name has changed a couple of times, it has always retained the symbolic acronym of its early days. Today, the Federation of Associations for the Integration of Homosexuality COC Nederland (N.V.I.H. COC) has branches in cities all over the Netherlands. The Amsterdam headquarters is around the corner from the Anne Frank House and the Homo Monument. COC offers a full schedule of support group meetings, workshops, socials, and party/disco nights for men and women, separate and mixed, with special events for gay seniors.

COFFEESHOPS

No exploration of the Red-Light District would be complete without venturing into a few of the coffeeshops. These are unique Dutch institutions and exemplify the rational, pragmatic attitude of the Dutch towards a social problem which is tearing other countries apart.

When I first visited Amsterdam in 1966, it was a far different city from the one you see today. Holland was still recovering from the effects of World War II at home and from expensive, unsuccessful attempts afterwards to retain her Asian empire, now Indonesia. The economy was strong, but this had not yet extended to the consumer sector. In the canal house where I lived, whoever was up first was responsible for the stoking of the coal-stove in the parlor, which was our only source of heat, and my landlady had been on the waiting list for a telephone for seven years! There were ladies in the windows in *de Wallen*, but most of them were Dutch, and I don't remember any of them in fluorescent underwear. It was a poor neighborhood, with rowdy saloons, basement drug dens, and gambling joints catering mostly to merchant seamen and local citizens, not tourists. The Boeing 747 had not yet brought affordable international travel to the masses; and the multitude of sex shops and such attractions as the Casa Rossa live sex shows, the dancing girls at the Bananenbar, the Erotic Museum, all those businesses aimed at today's enormous tourist trade, were just glimmers in the imaginations of young Amsterdam entrepreneurs. The traditional existence of openly tolerated prostitution, the loosening of social and sexual mores which accompanied the political upheavals of the late 1960s, and cheap air travel combined to turn *de Wallen* from just one of Holland's red-light districts (there are "window streets" in eleven cities in the country), where the ladies had been tolerated for centuries, into a major international tourist attraction.

And, of course, there were no coffeeshops. Although many of the people I met working and traveling around the continent were smoking hashish (marijuana was too bulky and risky to smuggle), there was not yet a policy of tolerance. People would buy matchboxes of hash in pubs, then step out into alleyways to smoke. The preferred

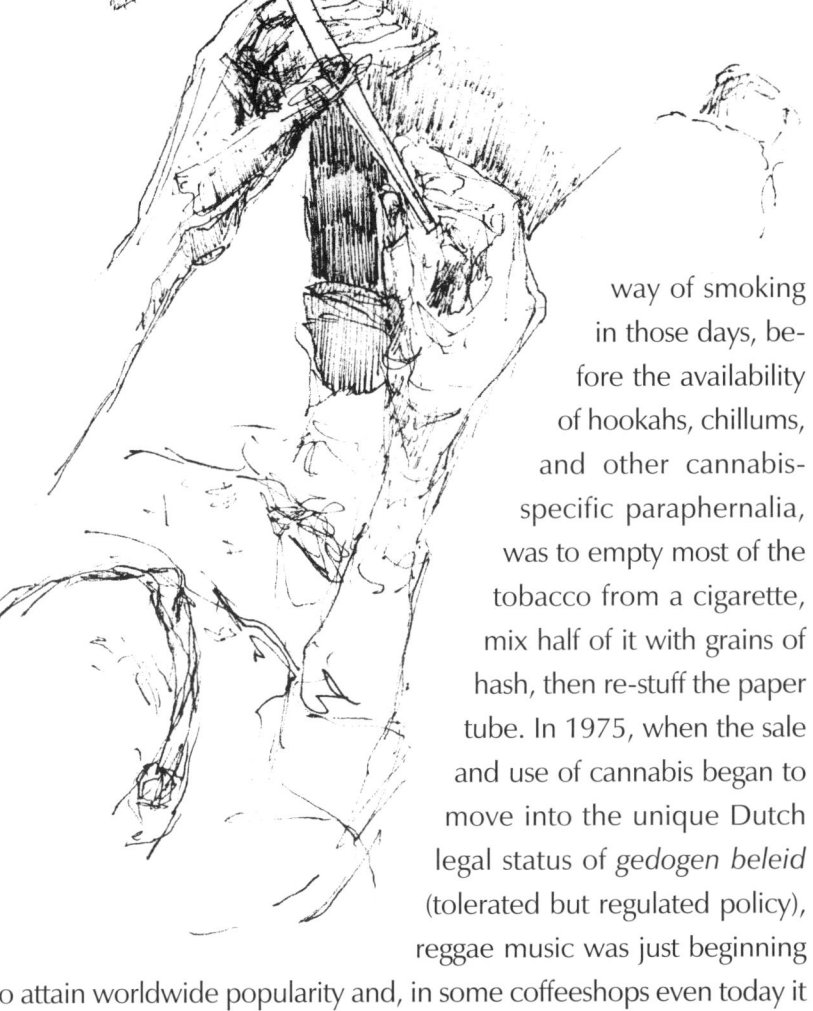

way of smoking in those days, before the availability of hookahs, chillums, and other cannabis-specific paraphernalia, was to empty most of the tobacco from a cigarette, mix half of it with grains of hash, then re-stuff the paper tube. In 1975, when the sale and use of cannabis began to move into the unique Dutch legal status of *gedogen beleid* (tolerated but regulated policy), reggae music was just beginning to attain worldwide popularity and, in some coffeeshops even today it seems as though Bob Marley must be the patron saint of Amsterdam. I believe the influence of the Jamaican Rastafarian spliff, and the earlier habit of mixing hash and tobacco together in Europe, came together to give birth to the "Dutch joint," usually about 40 percent cannabis.

After a generation of operating as licensed, regulated businesses, coffeeshops have now become an accepted part of Dutch daily life. The licensing of coffeeshops took an untaxed street business into the fold of the Dutch taxation and social welfare systems. The oldest continuous venue, the Bulldog, still occupies the pride of place at its original location in the heart of *de Wallen* and also operates at five other locations in the city, as well as at branches in Ibiza, Spain, and Vancouver, Canada. The Bulldog Palace, fronting on Leidseplein, was originally the headquarters of the Amsterdam police!

There are currently over 400 coffeeshops in the Netherlands, with nearly 300 of them in Amsterdam. Not surprisingly, the Red-Light District has more than its share. Contrary to popular opinion in many other parts of the world, Dutch coffeeshops, even in *de Wallen*, are not dingy, ill-lit, unsavory dope dens (although there are a few of those), but offer a wide range of goods, services, and ambience. You can sample the cannabis menu at a Country 'n' Western saloon right out of Bakersfield, "groove" in a psychedelic cafe, or smoke hashish in a typical 1950s American diner, complete to the jukebox consoles mounted on Formica-topped tables. Some sell alcohol, although licenses since 1995 have not been granted for both cannabis and booze. The rest all sell coffee, tea, and soft drinks. One can generally stave off the "munchies" with sweet snacks or a tasty *tosti* (toasted sandwich).

A typical menu will list several varieties of hash and weed, and most sell "space cakes," made with cannabis and other hemp-based products. The rules for the tolerated marijuana trade are rigid and enforced. Under the doctrine of *gedogen*, only possession and sale of up to five grams is permitted, and no coffeeshop may keep more than 500 grams in inventory. Persons under eighteen years of age are not

permitted in coffeeshops. If you ask where the stock comes from, you'll find that nobody knows! The cultivation and sale of commercial quantities is still illegal, and there are periodic raids on outdoor plantations and indoor "grow rooms" (rooms used for growing marijuana in an apartment, basement, or other location.) A great deal of the cannabis consumed in Amsterdam is grown in the Netherlands, using modern techniques of cultivation, cloning, and crossbreeding to yield a product of high quality and potency. Supplies for anything from a five-plant home garden (the tolerated limit for cultivation) to a plantation, including seeds, can be obtained at numerous "grow shops" (agricultural supply houses) throughout the city. A good deal of the supply still comes from North Africa, a traditional source of the drug for Europeans. Unlike fully legal businesses, if a coffeeshop is caught violating the terms of *gedogen*, it does not have a lot of legal recourse and, for a serious violation, may lose its license immediately and permanently.

Some other drugs are also tolerated in the Netherlands. There are several "smart shops" in the Red Light. These generally sell various strains and strengths of "magic" psychedelic mushrooms, to be ingested, smoked, or drunk as tea, as well as a wide range of herbal concoctions mimicking the effects of amphetamines, ecstasy, and other drugs illegal in their pure forms. Smart shops vary as much as coffeeshops. A lot of them are just straight retail outlets, albeit with an unusual inventory. One of the nicest in *de Wallen*, Conscious Dreams on Warmoesstraat, is spacious, bright, and airy. In addition to drugs, paraphernalia, and literature, the rear of the shop offers Internet access and a comfortable lounge overlooking the water, complete with a "brain machine" which, for €3, will take you on a virtual reality "trip" to induce a state of complete relaxation.

For information on the history of tolerated and persecuted drug use, a good stop is at Cannabis College, listed in the Source Directory at the back of this book. The founder, a pioneer cannabis activist, also owns the Flying Dutchman seed company, just across the canal—one of the first businesses devoted to supplying the needs of growers. Cannabis College is a nonprofit foundation dedicated to ending the war on drugs. Entry is free, and a small donation gains you admission to the lovely and fragrant basement "grow room," where you are free to take photographs.

If you are not a cannabis user, you need feel no compulsion to purchase or consume drugs in a coffeeshop. It is an entertaining experience just to relax with a drink and watch the wide variety of consumers of all ages, in jeans and business suits, fitting no common image of the furtive drug fiend, but rather representing a cross-section of the population in general. If you do partake, where else can you learn the art of rolling a Dutch joint?

It's hard for anyone aside from the most rabidly misinformed antidrug crusader to argue that the tolerance of cannabis use has been anything but a success. The law strictly prohibits the use of hard drugs, and these laws are rigorously enforced. The LSD, or Landelijk Steunpunt voor Drugsgebruikers (National Information Center for Drug Users), however, has proposed that the police extend *gedogen beleid* to include street corner dealers of psychedelics, on the grounds that, while these drugs drive normal people crazy, they calm down junkies, and such a policy would make the streets more peaceful, and the cops' jobs easier.

Most coffeeshops are mellow neighborhood hangouts which have, after a quarter-century, become an accepted, if not universally approved of, part of the normal mix of urban service industries. When Holland and Belgium jointly hosted the Euro-Cup 2000 soccer championships, it was suggested that the operations of coffeeshops in Amsterdam be curtailed. The idea was laughed down, and there were no incidents of football (soccer) hooliganism during the games here, just huge, loud, good-humored street parties. The Amsterdam *politie* even published an informative and humorous brochure illustrating the rules and regulations of the Red-Light District. In Belgium, which has since begun the process of decriminalizing cannabis, fans stoked on Belgian

beers running from 8–12 percent alcohol clashed with a police force which had invested a fortune in riot gear, water cannons, and detention facilities. The result was a predictably bloody riot which resulted in hundreds of injuries and arrests, and mass deportations of (mostly British) hooligans.

GAMBLING IN THE RED LIGHT

So-called "fruit machines" have been a fixture of Dutch pub life for many years. When I first visited Amsterdam in the sixties, every local pub had a couple of these small slot machines, which featured small wagers and payoffs, even though gambling was illegal. With increasing prosperity and disposable income, the Dutch wanted more, and *de Wallen* became a center for illegal gambling dens offering card games and, in Chinatown, oriental tiles. In the 1970s, as tourism began to transform the Red Light, the Dutch characteristically set up foundations to study the social costs of prostitution, gambling, and cannabis. When it was determined that the population wanted liberalization of gambling laws, the Holland Casino Stichting was empowered to create a uniformly managed chain of full casinos so that the Dutch could enjoy Roulette, Punto Banco, Blackjack, and American-style electronic slot machines. The intent was, and is, to provide all citizens with conveniently located places to play, assured of comfort, security, and honest games.

The first Holland Casino opened in 1975 at Scheveningen, a coastal resort city near the capital, the eleventh of the planned twelve total venues opened in Utrecht in 2000. Although these casinos offer the "only legal gambling in Holland," you will find slot machine casinos scattered all over the country, ranging from cubbyhole storefronts to the huge Arcade Casino on Amsterdam's Damrak. There are a half-dozen places to play *spelautomaten* (slot machines) in the Red-Light District, but these days the stakes and potential wins (and losses) can be much greater than in my youth. I've seen customers in small pubs put hundreds of euros into these electronic bandits in the course of an afternoon. If you decide to use one of these *spelautomaten,* ask an attendant for advice before you play; the games are different and seem more complicated than the American casino slots you'll find at Holland Casino Amsterdam. There is also a bingo parlor in the Red Light and, not far away, on Rembrandtsplein, the Casino Femina, which offers roulette and blackjack in direct competition with the official casino.

The only time I've heard of Holland Casino going to court to protect its monopoly was when a Vienna-based casino chain opened an American-style poker club in Amsterdam, claiming that they didn't violate the monopoly because poker is not a gambling game. They lost. However, as soon as Holland Casino has opened its twelfth casino, the plan has been, from the outset, to open up Dutch gambling to competition from the private sector, which will result in many of the existing local operations being moving from *gedoogd* to completely legal.

If gambling is one of your pleasures, be sure to stop in at a couple of Red-Light casinos, but don't miss Holland Casino Amsterdam, right off Leidesplein. This is a beautifully and elegantly appointed place to visit, and features one of the best restaurants in the city. Even if you're not a player, admission (normally €3.50) is free on Wednesdays, and you'll get a coupon for a free drink at the bar.

The one "gamble" you don't want to take in *de Wallen* is *balletje-balletje,* which was mentioned earlier. Particularly as the weather warms, you'll see fast-talking hustlers kneeling in the alleys, shuffling three matchboxes around on a square of carpet, defying bettors to find which box hides the little white ball. Stand and watch for a while, and you'll see hundreds of euros bet on this, possibly the world's oldest street con. There are, of course, three or more confederates of the "dealer" in the crowd, pumping up the action, beating the game, until the one sucker they're playing finally plunks down his bet. You cannot beat this game! An acquaintance of mine tried, by putting his foot on the box he thought hid the ball instead of pointing, as etiquette demands. He was correct on the placement of the ball. But, when he demanded to be paid off, the dealer's "shills" surrounded him menacingly until their leader could disappear with carpet, matchboxes, ball, and of course, my friend's money. The oldest con game and the oldest profession exist together in *de Wallen!*

THE SALESMEN

De *Wallen* is full of salesmen of all types. The Red Light is a neighborhood, and you'll find almost every sort of legitimate business tucked in among the more shocking enterprises: hardware stores, dry cleaners, local pubs, tobacco shops, and snack bars. The area has everything a resident could need.

There are other salesmen as well. On the streets leading into the Red Light, and in the alleyways within, you'll encounter small groups hawking baking soda as cocaine or aspirin as ecstasy. Be advised, your chances of scoring real hard drugs on the streets of Amsterdam are only slightly better than finding your true love in one of the windows. Coffeeshops, at least, ensure that naive visitors are not sold oregano as marijuana.

Although they try hard to look and come on like rap video thugs, these characters are more pathetic than threatening, mostly junkies, burnouts, and cheap hustlers. I will, though, give them credit for being able to stand on those frigid street corners for hours every day in the dead of an Amsterdam winter. If you are accosted by one of the street "dealers," just walk on by and ignore him, and you won't usually be further hassled. There is little violent stranger-to-stranger crime in Amsterdam, although a tourist wandering drunk in de Wallen in the wee hours may, by appearing vulnerable, steel the nerves of one of the groups of young street punks sufficient to provoke a robbery. The most common offense against tourists is pickpocketing, particularly in the crowds around the central railway station and in the Red Light.

Of course, while the younger, more gullible visitors are waiting for the ecstasy high or cocaine rush which will never come, the Red Light has a resident population, in flophouses and on the street, of real junkies who require real drugs. They'll run any hustle they can on unsuspecting tourists, or each other, to raise the cash to score. I was once sitting in the open window of a coffeeshop on the Nieuwmarkt as two "salesmen" were conducting a negotiation on the sidewalk outside. They were flashing what looked like cheap watches and jewelry at one another, behaving alternately pugnacious and brotherly, and weaving slightly. Two other customers were also enjoying their slapstick attempts at dignified commerce when the barmaid suddenly exclaimed, "They are two thieves, trying to rob each other!" Our laughter drew their attention and they turned, managed to look embarrassed for their unexpected audience, and shuffled off into the adjacent alley. When all the day's loot is converted to cash, it will be turned over to the real dealers—the guardians of the True Fix—in alleys tourists rarely enter.

Screens

When they're not on the hustle, you'll often see addicts huddled together in the alleyways, two or three ragged souls inspecting the quantity and quality of an aluminium foil "bindle."

The Dutch do not regard addiction in itself as a crime, but a disease (the Dutch word for addict, *verslaafde*, translates as "enslaved one"). Junkies are not subject to much persecution (except when they get caught dealing) but are served by numerous government-sponsored treatment programs and a free clean-needle exchange for those who inject. Many, however, prefer to smoke, and the same pipe screens used for hashish serve as well for efficient consumption of heroin or cocaine. Licensed *horeca* (hospitality) businesses in Amsterdam are officially encouraged not to serve addicts. Coffeeshops also discourage a junkie clientele, but many will sell them screens, so long as they don't stick around or try to sneak into the toilets. Some are already so "on the nod" when they come in that they'll pass into a trance state at the bar, money in hand, and have to be roused and reminded of their mission.

If you are a "drug tourist" here to buy something harder than cannabis, mushrooms, or "smart" drugs, and wish to avoid wasting your money and risking an unpleasant encounter with the normally mellow Amsterdam *politie*, again I urge you to *ignore the street dealers*. Real hard drugs are available, often in the city's many dance clubs,

but even there you will be buying from a stranger and may be victimized.

Another Dick in the Joker

Addicts from many lands get lost in the Red-Light District. When they are too far gone to make it on some kind of street hustle, they'll often sneak into crowded coffeeshops and, once inside, try to look "helpful" by working the tables, emptying ashtrays, while cadging coins and cigarettes from the customers. Once in, if they are marginally presentable and don't smell too rank, many counterpersons will let them make one or two circuits of the room, then order them out. This Englishman ("another dick in the Joker") was trying such a dodge, totally oblivious to his total exposure. He stood, swaying on the support of his cane, the tourists agape at his equipment swaying in tempo. It took the barmaid ten minutes to get him out the door, protesting all the way. Even in *de Wallen,* there are some taboos.

DE POLITIE

If you have the good fortune to see the Amsterdam/Amstelland police in action on the streets, you'll see law-enforcement work based on very different tactics and strategies than those used in any other city in the world. First of all, the Dutch abolished the height requirement for officers some years ago, and many of the men and women in blue seem better-sized for careers as jockeys than as cops. This, and the generally laid-back attitudes of these public servants, makes the *politie* an almost unobtrusive presence on the streets of Amsterdam. I have heard visitors remark that they hadn't seen any police in the Red Light. In fact, they just overlooked the patrols, on foot and bicycle, in VW mini-cruisers and on horseback, that range through *de Wallen* constantly. The almost unmilitary design of their often-rumpled uniforms also helps them blend into the bustling crowds of visitors and citizens.

When there are confrontations, the police work as a well-trained team with, it seems, one prime directive: "Don't scare the tourists!" Brawlers, drunks, and rowdies who, anywhere else, would be beaten bloody in the course of arrest, are instead treated with respect, coddled along, and calmed down by a sympathetic officer, so another part of the team can sneak up behind the malefactor and snap the cuffs on. The offender is usually so shamefaced at being taken in so easily that there is no further problem whisking him into a Black Mariah for a quick trip to the cells. I saw a fight ended and arrest made on Rembrandtsplein one night. The police team consisted of seven officers by the time the cuffs went on. Anywhere else, two bluecoats with night sticks could have handled the situation in minutes, loudly and bloodily. The brawl had attracted a crowd of about fifty tourists, including a group of chattering Japanese. The tactics used meant that the entire scenario took twenty minutes, but there was no blood on the pavement, and the crowd dispersed in a good mood, having witnessed an exciting incident without feeling any sense of personal danger.

With more passive problems, the *politie* have an even more passive strategy. I observed such a case in the heart of the Red Light. In the middle of an alley, a working-class North African was screaming at a young blonde in one of the windows, and she was giving it right back, supported by a chorus of her colleagues leaning out of their own windows. Two officers were already on the scene. Their first tactic was to change the focus of the man's attention from the girl to them. Argument is a national sport in the Netherlands, and the opportunity to

voice his grievance to the authorities calmed the man down considerably. But he was still pretty loud after he'd gotten across to the police and the amused spectators that he hadn't been satisfied with the fifteen minutes he'd had with the blonde, and thought he deserved five more! The officers patiently waited him out. Then, when they were sure there was no further risk of violence, they started to inch their way down the alley to the next street, backs half-turned to the complaining customer. It took about a minute before he realized he had lost his audience as the cops disappeared around the corner, the crowd drifted away, and the girls went back inside their window rooms and back to work. He was almost alone on the street and, with an embarrassed look, shrugged his shoulders and went on his way.

The above incident was as amusing for the actions of the ladies in the windows as for the comedy of the "confrontation." Prostitutes are women, like any others. On a quiet afternoon, you'll see them leaning out of their open windows, chatting and gossiping with each other, their "boyfriends," or passing acquaintances. Sometimes, when something outrageous happens, all the girls not entertaining clients will rush into the street and converge on the action, giggling just like schoolgirls, but *very* out of uniform!

Of course, the drug policies in the Netherlands present unusual problems and situations for peace officers. Many foreigners have difficulty understanding that the laws against hard drugs are rigorously enforced, not least because they see so many "dealers" on the streets of the Red Light openly hawking cocaine, heroin, and ecstasy. I met an American who is a devotee of "magic" mushrooms, which can be openly purchased in "smart shops." On his first night in town, the young tourist was approached by a panhandling junkie in *de Wallen*. He gave the man some change and was immediately grabbed by two

patrolling officers, who demanded his passport and that he empty his pockets. When they found out that all he had was a baggy of dried "shrooms," they apologized, telling him they thought he'd been making a "coke" buy. They politely returned his legal drugs and let him go, cautioning him never to buy hard drugs on the street as almost all of the product is fake, and you run the real risk of arrest. He'll be back.

If you have a problem of any sort in the Red Light—with dealers, prostitutes, pimps, or other denizens—do not hesitate to approach a police officer. They all speak English, and nothing you tell them will surprise or shock them. The general emergency number in Amsterdam is 112. There are two police stations convenient to *de Wallen,* on Beursstraat, on the west side of the Red Light, and to the east, on Keizersgracht (near the Nieuwmarkt).

Many visitors to Amsterdam don't take much note of the police, either because of their relatively low profile, or because they come from places in which the relationship between law enforcement and citizenry is one of apprehension and distrust, and hesitate to draw attention to themselves. But, as we've seen, the unusual tactics and appearance of the Amsterdam/Amstelland police, and the generally mutual respect between them and the people they serve, make observing law enforcement in action one of the city's more interesting and entertaining attractions for visitors. And, if you get carried away in the Red Light and seriously ignore the rules, a foreign passport will not necessarily save you a trip to the cells, but you will get there in one piece!

DIFFERENT STROKES

Prostitution Elsewhere

As we've mentioned, Amsterdam is only one of eleven cities in the Netherlands with public *raamstraten*—and there are two other, smaller, less flashy red-light districts in the capital itself. My young friend Jules van Harn swears that he has passed through a small "one-whore town," where the only window's curtain was closed, not for a customer, but by display of a sign reading, "NOZ (*Niet op zondag*: Not on Sunday)." But, Jules is, as I've mentioned, a brash young man, and may well be pulling my leg. You will, however, find porno shops and sex clubs operating in, and *tippelaars* working the streets of, towns throughout the country. These do not have otherwise sanctioned areas for open practice of the trade. Several other cities have also established official *tippelzones* similar to the one in Amsterdam.

Unless you are a dedicated "sex tourist," you probably won't want to visit a *tippelzone* in Amsterdam or anywhere else or to take a long trip to compare red-light districts. However, there are areas of window brothels in two cities close to Amsterdam. In Haarlem, fifteen minutes by train from the central station, you'll find ladies in the windows surrounding that city's large Gothic church. Just a thirty-minute journey away, in Utrecht, which was the most important city in Holland before the fifteenth-century rise of Amsterdam, the window brothels in one of its two red-light districts are on houseboats.

The Amsterdam areas have traditionally provided refuge for religious exiles from elsewhere in Europe. The Sephardic Jews who came from Spain and Portugal after the expulsions of 1492 were later joined by Ashkenazi co-religionists from Eastern Europe and assimilated to become an important segment of Amsterdam culture and commerce. Similarly, Protestant Huguenots fleeing French persecution repaid Dutch hospitality by contributions to their adopted homeland. The English Puritans, America's Pilgrim Fathers, however, accepted sanctuary in Amsterdam, Haarlem, and Leiden for just twelve years. Then, fearing that their children were being corrupted by liberal local attitudes, they sailed away in 1620 to land on Plymouth Rock and bring America the most unDutch spectacle of the Salem witch trials. Perhaps the *raamvrouwen* of Haarlem had something to do with it.

Central Station

Other Amsterdam Red-Light Areas: Spuistraat

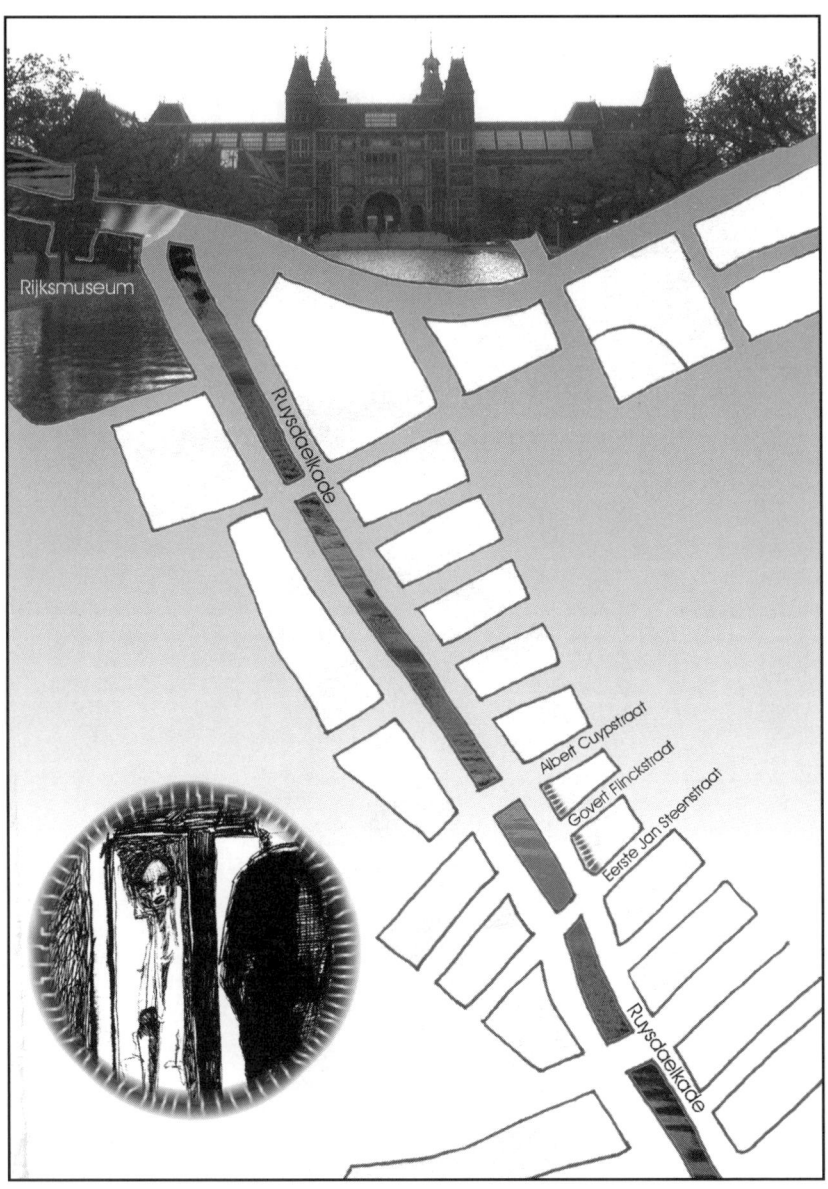

Other Amsterdam Red-Light Areas: Ruysdaelkade

Porn in the Mass Media

Although the Dutch tolerate open prostitution, this does not mean that parents brag about how well their daughters are doing in the windows. And, although some of the hard-core pornography so openly available in the Red-Light shops is available at every newsstand, selections usually exclude the roughest publications. The attitude toward sex is that it is a natural need, and that, therefore, the Dutch have as much right to a satisfying sex life as to the exercise of any other of their basic freedoms. Dutch citizens with qualifying disabilities are even entitled to government benefits covering the services of sex workers!

Where sex is considered a natural practice, in all forms, curiosity about it is not discouraged, and members of the mass media in the Netherlands are permitted to satisfy that curiosity as explicitly as they wish. If you visit a bar or coffeeshop in the Red Light, you'll usually find a selection of local magazines, subscribed to by the management for their patrons. Two of the most popular are *Panorama* and *Aktueel,* either of which you can also read at any public library. Leafing through these publications, you'll find explicit cartoons, sexual advice columns, and reader letters dealing with sex and other bodily functions which would be unprintable outside the pages of *Hustler* magazine in the United States. Recent feature articles covered the woman with the world's longest nipples (4 cm), the life of a hard-working twenty-five-year-old *tippelaar* in Tilburg, and a lady who sells dominant sex to other ladies at the five-star brothel Yab Yum. Both magazines also run pictorials of attractive, normally employed young ladies, undressed, but presented tastefully, on a par with *Playboy*, accompanied by brief interviews focusing on "her first time" or best-ever sexual experience.

Busking

There are street entertainers all over town year-round, but, in the high season, Amsterdam is a magnet for hundreds of buskers from all over the world: musicians, jugglers, living statues, caricaturists, any sort of divertissement which may separate a passing tourist from a few euros. Walking through the Red Light, you may encounter a Peruvian folk band, a Kentucky bluegrass quartet, or a Russian vocal orchestra. There are even a few motivated street people who sing on the street, unaccompanied, croaking off-key standards with junk-cracked voices, but who must elicit some sympathy from passersby or they wouldn't be there everyday. Much of the street entertainment is surprisingly professional. Many of the performers also work clubs and have released CDs but find busking a welcome supplement to more stable local income or a great way to pay for a vacation in Amsterdam. The narrow, crowded streets of de Wallen are, unfortunately, unsuitable for some of the more dramatic acts, such as the Aussie who juggles two operating chain saws from atop a ten-foot unicycle. You'll usually find these novelty acts playing the Leidseplein, in front of the Bulldog Palace.

AFTERWORD

With *Closed Curtain*, we have attempted to produce a synergy between Michelle's visual and my written observations of the "lives of *de Wallen.*" We have not attempted to address in depth the profound social, sexual, and political issues raised by the open acceptance in the Netherlands of businesses and behavior which many people feel undermine the very foundations of public morality, even of Western civilization itself. This is a subjective work; readers who feel

we've painted either too upbeat or gloomy a picture of the
Red Light may both be right. But,
if you are still reading at this point,
we'll assume you found our efforts
entertaining, and that we have increased your enjoyment and
understanding of one of Europe's most unusual and exciting
tourist attractions, *de Wallen* in Amsterdam. Beyond its tawdry
and shocking aspects, this is a living community, a visual delight, an ar-
chitectural treasure trove, and a major crossroads of European culture
and commerce that has thrived for eight centuries.

SOURCE DIRECTORY

I f your interests run more deeply, we conclude *Closed Curtain* with the following list of sources you may consult on Dutch attitudes and policies towards prostitution, *de Wallen*, drugs, and gays. In a country run by consensus, with twelve different major political parties, it's not surprising that there is a *stichting*, or activist group, involved in virtually every issue, so we haven't attempted to be comprehensive.

Mr A. de Graaf Stichting
Westermarkt 4
1016 DK Amsterdam
020 624 7149
www.mrgraaf.nl
A government-funded foundation that advises on issues of prostitution and promotes public awareness of them. The foundation was instrumental in the complete decriminalization of the sex industries in October 2000. Visits by appointment only.

Stichting de Rode Draad
Kloveniersburgwal 47
1011 JX Amsterdam
020 624 3366
www.rodedraad.nl
The Red Thread is the "prostitutes' union," advising sex workers on their rights and social welfare benefits. It publishes *Black Light*, a magazine for prostitutes which is also sold to the public. Visits by appointment only.

Prostitution Information Center
Enge Kerksteeg 3
1012 GV Amsterdam
020 420 7328
www.pic-amsterdam.com
Run by a former sex worker, the P.I.C. is a major source of information for prostitutes, their clients, and the general public. Open to the public, but hours are limited, so it's best to call before you visit.

Rob van Hulst Productie
Zeedijk 34
1012 AZ Amsterdam
020 624 5720
www.redlight-tours.com
Psychologist/author/actor Rob van Hulst has lived in and studied the Red Light for over 20 years. His tour company offers a wide variety of tours of de Wallen.

De Wallenmanager
The Wallen Manager
020 522 4377
The position of Wallen manager was created to help in the ongoing city effort to improve the liveability of the Red Light. It is a source for information on municipal services with the motto: "A liveable Wallen district? Why not help too? Together we can do it!" This is an effort even visitors can support.

Condomerie
Warmoesstraat 141 H/S
1012 JB Amsterdam
020 627 4174
www.condomerie.com
Condomerie was founded in 1987 as a response to the AIDS epidemic and is devoted to promoting safe sex through condom use. Here you can find information and literature, advice on the right condom for you, and a wide variety of "fun and fantasy" creations.

Cannabis College Stichting
Oudezijds Achterburgwal 124
1012 DT Amsterdam
020 423 4420
www.cannabiscollege.com
Established by one of the pioneers of Dutch cannabis horticulture, Cannabis College is dedicated to ending the war on drugs. Free admission.

Museum Hennep Hasj
Oudezijds Achterburgwal 130
1012 DV Amsterdam.
020 623 5961
The Hemp Hash Museum offers exhibits showing the cultivation and preparation of hashish, industrial uses of hemp, books, & souvenirs.

COC-Nederland
Postbus 3836
Rozenstraat 14
1001 AP Amsterdam
020 623 4596
www.coc.nl
The most important, largest, and oldest organization for gays and lesbians in the Netherlands, with 31 regional departments.

Amsterdams Historisch Museum
Nieuwezijds Voorburgwal 359
1012 RM Amsterdam
020 523 1822
The Amsterdam Historical Museum is probably the least-visited (by tourists) of the city's cultural destinations. It's not in de Wallen, but if you want to know how the city developed over time, there is no better source of information—and you won't have to wait in line!

INDEX

White-Boucke publishes general non-fiction books (many of a humorous nature) and specialized reference media.

WHITE-BOUCKE PUBLISHING, INC.
PO BOX 400
LAFAYETTE, CO 80026, USA
tel: (303) 604-0661
fax: (303) 604-0662
e-mail: ordering@white-boucke.com

Our full range of books, videotapes and CD-ROMs can also be found on our Internet website:

http://www.white-boucke.com